Love is in This Room

MEMORIES OF TEACHING SPECIAL KIDS

LAUREL LORRAINE LANCER, PhD.

Copyright © 2022 Laurel Lorraine Lancer, PhD.

All rights reserved. No part of this book may be reproduced, stored, or transmitted by any means—whether auditory, graphic, mechanical, or electronic—without written permission of both publisher and author, except in the case of brief excerpts used in critical articles and reviews. Unauthorized reproduction of any part of this work is illegal and is punishable by law.

ISBN: 979-8-88640-112-7 (sc)
ISBN: 979-8-88640-113-4 (hc)
ISBN: 979-8-88640-114-1 (e)

Because of the dynamic nature of the Internet, any web addresses or links contained in this book may have changed since publication and may no longer be valid. The views expressed in this work are solely those of the author and do not necessarily reflect the views of the publisher, and the publisher hereby disclaims any responsibility for them.

One Galleria Blvd., Suite 1900, Metairie, LA 70001
1-888-421-2397

*In Memory of
Valerie Holladay*

CONTENTS

Acknowledgments vii
Introduction ix

Chapter 1 Gentler Times 1
    Interviews 3
    O.K. 4
    If She Says So 5
    Sally's Keeper 7

Chapter 2 History of the Special Programs 11

Chapter 3 The Early Program for the Emotionally Disturbed ... 15

Chapter 4 My Classrooms of Emotionally Disturbed 23

Chapter 5 My "Crazy" Boys 29
    The Bully 29
    Military School 32
    Grandmothers 34
    "Say Yeah" 36
    Three Bird Day 39
    Karma? 43
    I Am In Charge 45
    Red 48
    I'm Sorry 50
    Picasso 52
    Expletives 56

Chapter 6 Working With The Learning Disabled 59

Chapter 7 My LD Kids 64
    Looking Normal 64

  I Fell 66
  Choose Me 68
  Bouncing 72
  To Feel Better 76
  A Future Great Poet 78
  Only If I'm Paid 82
  The Children's Hour 86
  Lost Baby 90
  Sandy's Courage 93
  The Vale Brothers 96
  Climb a Tree 97
  A Model Student 99
  I'm Not So Bad 101
  Not *My* Flag 105
  Rainbow Dreams 106
  Bounty Hunter 108
  Being Normal 113
  Young Tutor 115
  Names 119
  An Over Achiever? 121
  Entertain Me 123
  Red Eye 124
  "Thank You!" 126

Chapter 8 Wanting A Real Family 131

Chapter 9 Our Own Keystone Cops? 146

Chapter 10 My "Special" Adults 150
  Anne 151
  Kathy 151
  Gary 152
  Rosie 154
  Dr. HUGE 155
  Linda S. 157
  Mr. C 159

Jeff	161
Dick	163
Linda P	165
Liz	166
Sarah	168

Chapter 11 Post-Mortem **172**
    My Volunteer Kids 173
    Rubie 174
    I Have All Four 176
    I'm Good At This 179

Chapter 12 Summary **181**

Chapter 13 Heart **183**
    Roseann 183
    Shannon 184
    Jacob 186
    Final Say 189
    Students In My Volunteer Classes 191

ACKNOWLEDGMENTS

I would like to give credit to all the beautiful children that have touched my life. This book is a series of stories about some of my most memorable students and associates in education. The stories are all true. The dialogue is often correct as it was spoken. I did take some notes over the years so that I have some specific records of exactly what was said. In many cases the meaning and intent are accurate and the words are as I can most closely recall them. I have changed some names in order to protect those identities. Most of the adult's names are changed, and some of the children's. The decision on whether or not to change a name depended on the number of years that have passed since the event, and also the severity of the person's individual problems. I had difficulty speaking of my young friends using a different name. Their names seem to be part of their personalities.

I must acknowledge the help that my personal faith has given me to continue working with children over the years. My belief in God and in His Son, Jesus Christ, have sustained me through many difficulties. I need to acknowledge that I prayerfully approached my assignments of teaching with a daily prayer that the Holy Spirit would influence me to give the needed attention to each child, and that I could lovingly and intelligently enlist my knowledge to correctly approach my method of teaching to best meet the needs of the special deficits that impaired my students. I hope that my influence on these lovely kids has been for the good. I do know that my relationships with them have proven enlightening, faith promoting, and personally fulfilling to me for many wonderful years.

I would like to give a special thanks to my dear niece, Natalie Scherlong, who stepped in at the last minute to be my new editor. She has been extremely helpful. My wonderful, past editor, Valerie Holladay, succumbed to cancer just a few months ago. She was still agreeing to assist me—even when she was quite ill.

I wish to acknowledge the support given to me by my family in writing this, and the encouragement of friends (particularly one dear friend who reminded me of all the readers that would wish to see my book). Also I wish to mention the patience of my family as I continued in the educational system for so long a tenure. I loved all of the children, most of the "classified" help, some of the fellow teachers, and a few of the administrators. I am still enjoying the companionship of students, as I volunteer at my old school instructing in creative writing. I hope that you, the reader, will enjoy my tales of very interesting and unforgettable children.

INTRODUCTION

How fortunate I was to teach school when I did. I began in the late-fifties and have just recently retired. I taught elementary school for about forty-five years, and the education system has dramatically changed in America. In the early history of public elementary schools there was a one room schoolhouse supported by the community. The teacher was the instructor, disciplinarian, custodian, and property manager. He/she needed to come early, build a fire if needed, maintain the cleanliness of the building, raise the level of education of his/her pupils, and be responsible for the behavior of the students in his/her care.

Jump ahead to the present and we see great differences, for better and for worse. The teacher now arrives to spend an hour in a planning meeting, is instructed on how to present each lesson, has a paraprofessional to mind the students during recess, before and after school, and during lunchtime. The teachers have become robots, teaching each lesson in the same manner and language—just like the other teacher down the hall. There is no creativity or initiative and the process is very cold and impersonal.

I had the best of times. We were given a course of study for the year, told what subjects and skills needed to be taught, and given a lesson plan book and access to a closet that had several cabinets with some materials. We were supposed to fill out the lesson plan weekly, although many teachers did not and were unmonitored.

We could schedule the amount of time we were spending on each subject, get what materials we wanted to use to supplement texts or for our own interest, and we were in total charge of teaching that particular grade level. As a new teacher, I did ask for advice from the more experienced teachers. Most of all the instruction for the children was more personal, more individualized, and we were more involved with the students.

After many years of experience and, I feel, success, I believe that the most important ingredient in being a good teacher is the ability to connect with the student. I had this connection with my students and the rewards were very great. I made close friendships with many students and have kept in touch with some well into their adult lives. Children know when you care. I feel it is very important that students know that their teacher cares about them, and really desires that they be able to learn. This personal connection was vital to me and I feel that in the current teaching atmosphere, caring has no place and is actually discouraged. Individuality and personal involvement of teacher/student is almost a thing of the past. We no longer have "teachers", they are more accurately called "facilitators", and the system is more like something one would expect in a third world country.

With the federal government so involved in education, and the growth of small school districts causing them to become large bureaucracies, the control of education is no longer local. The lack of local regional control has made for a lot of national movements from less than brilliant idealists in education. Someone somewhere decided that, to improve the teaching, the teachers need to have someone to observe and mentor them. This became a national movement. In my district the "coaches", as they were called, were selected from the pets of the individual principals and /or higher administration officials. Many of those chosen were mentoring teachers far more qualified than themselves. In my school a counselor, who had never taught a classroom at all, became mentor to three very qualified fifth grade teachers with much more tenure than she, and the teachers were better at their jobs. The counselor had been less than effective at her own job, but was of a "minority race" and a favorite of the current principal. The year before

I retired, I witnessed three different teachers brought to tears from the interviews with the coaches after their observations. These coaches were neither educationally qualified, nor held appropriate training to counsel with their peers. The coaching program is still in effect, for some eight years now, and is costing the school district a lot of money.

Another national movement, is to employ superintendents who have no background in education, but have a background in the business field. This might be valid for an assistant superintendent in order to assist with monetary concerns of the district, but I have seen dire consequences from decisions made by some of these business experienced executives. One superintendent came through our school on a "walk through". This was another ill advised innovation for the district. A "walk through" consisted of a group of administrators, a school board member, and a parent all descending upon a classroom in session, and afterward meeting to discuss what they had observed. The school holding the walk through was in a semi "lock down". No one was to use the conference or media instruction rooms during that time. Large amounts of fancy treats were obtained from the central cafeteria department. All the faculty were "on their toes". One teacher had stayed until eight P.M. the prior evening getting her room ready for the ominous "walk through". She was plastering her wall with posters of information about writing procedures, math instructions, "word walls" (another innovation from the district involving lists of words for a unit of instruction), and other paraphernalia. The principal held a faculty meeting before school began on the "walk through" day. She had all of the teachers walk down to the classroom, that was so nicely prepared, and observe what a wonderful sight the visitors were going to see. The principal made the mistake of directing her question to *me*. "Well, what do you think?" I felt physically attacked by all the visual stimuli, and responded that my children (I was teaching highly distract-able learning disabled students) would react as I felt. I covered my head for protection and said that it was overwhelming and had too much "stuff". I felt it looked as if the teacher had put up various posters for instruction starting in the fall and had never removed anything all year. The principal was upset at my response and made no further comments. The others seemed uncomfortable and excused themselves to go to work.

The truth about the very "busy" classrooms was that the teachers were all told to cover their surfaces with instructional information. The windows were covered as were the the heating vents, the doors, and most surfaces in the class rooms. Two of the first grade teachers complained to me (one had to be careful about to whom complaints were made!) that they felt impeded in their instruction. They said that the classrooms felt too busy and had too much clutter. We all discussed how we should call the fire department and ask them to intervene. Those same two first grade teachers were gone the following year to a more reasonable and smaller school district.

Well, the impressive visitors came for the morning, and the superintendent stuck his head in the room across from mine. The fourth grade teacher there had just ten minutes between her students' return from music class and their scheduled lunch period. She wisely thought to use those few minutes to have the students practice their multiplication tables. She handed out sheets for a quick drill. WRONG. The superintendent went directly to the principals' office, demanded that the fourth grade teacher have a comment on her evaluation suggesting that she improve her instruction. His concern was, "We do not *practice* in school. School is for instruction". One would wonder if he understood the sequence of learning.

This is one example of a business executive running an educational institution. These folks do not have any background in educational processes, or learning theories. This same superintendent gave strong reprimands to the kindergarten teachers for teaching the "alphabet song". His edict was that we should not teach the letters in order. One would also wonder when the children would learn that, or would they grow up and have to have their computers alphabetize for them? This same educational leader proclaimed that *"All* students must have one year growth for one year in the program". I did ask my supervisor, "What happened to the old 'Bell Curve' that explained intelligence levels?" I suppose the students in the "life skills" (severely retarded) program should progress at the same level as those in the "gifted and talented" programs. This is truly a lock-step approach to education. Other mistakes were; the "whole language" program, which pulled out language as a separate area of instruction, and removed all language instruction texts from the classrooms (one copy left in the library for teacher reference), removal of grade level spelling lists from the district, new innovative readers that were not leveled for reading ability, use of "trade books" for reading instruction, use of journals only, for language instruction, and finally the removal of the teaching of cursive writing.

This superintendent had a rather short tenure and was followed by one whose background was in the military. Things are not much better, although the spelling lists are back.

I have been retired for a few years and continue to teach literature to a selected group of advanced students as a volunteer project, and I see some of the problems becoming more obvious. The students are less advanced academically, have poor spelling skills, have an inability to read or write cursive, have poor written and oral language skills, and exhibit excessive discipline problems. I am particularly concerned about the lack of personal interaction with students and teachers. I also am concerned that teachers no longer have the students say the Pledge of Allegiance at the start of the day. In addition, there are no longer American flags in each classroom.

I guess that I retired at a good time. I miss regular teaching, but it has changed so that I would have much difficulty adjusting to these new expectations. This last year I taught cursive writing to my fourth and fifth grade students to whom I gave my volunteer time. We do need smaller school districts, more local control, and escape from federal innovations. It now seems almost impossible to reverse some of the damage to education.

I am writing my book as a tribute to the old values in education, and to my beloved students who made my experience so wonderful. A short explanation for the title of my book is this little story:

I was teaching a learning disabled child in a hallway closet that had a table, several chairs, and a portable chalkboard. The principal called me to an important phone call. I told the little girl to complete her paper and I should return shortly. If I did not come back before the bell rang (indicating a change in classes) she should go on back to her classroom. The bell rang. I returned to the empty room and found this sweet note on the chalkboard. "Love is in this room, because Mrs Lancer is in this room." I was inspired by this for the rest of my career and it still pleases me to remember it to this day.

I hope you will enjoy the stories of the many children for whom I have great love.

> There was an old woman who taught in the schools,
> She had many poor children who'd not follow rules.
> She helped them to learn and deal with their dread.
> Some had been spanked soundly, but she loved them instead.

Chapter One

GENTLER TIMES

When I first started teaching, teaching itself was a surprise to me. I had not planned on teaching and disliked any and all education classes that I had taken at the university. I was an art major and wished to be a famous painter or sculptor. Educational classes were to be of assistance if ever I needed to make a hard living.

There were four of us close friends in college, all working our way through a state university some fifty miles away from our home. During the summer we needed to find employment in the city where we lived, in order to earn money again for the fall session. Sally was the one who would pay to go to the employment office and find where the companies were that were hiring. She would call the other three of us and let us know where she had obtained work. We would then go where Sally was and also apply for work. This was somewhat unfair to the employment agencies, but saved poor students from paying additional employment fees. We, of course, needed to pretend not to know one another—especially Sally—until we had been working together for a while. We shared numerous jobs at a phone company, a credit bureau, a bank, and a transportation company, all during the summers we were in college.

After graduation, Sally, who had trained as a teacher, had gotten a contract with a local school district and began teaching grade four in an elementary school. I was unhappily working at a title guaranty company and learning how to do house closings. She phoned me to let me know that they were in great need of new teachers in her school. They were adding an addition on to the building and a position would be available very soon. I had all the required college courses, but had not taken student teaching. The school district arranged with the state university to have me take student teaching at Sally's school while working with the first grade teachers there. I was so lucky as I was paid from the time I started working there, and I was also getting credit for student teaching. The education professor from the university drove to my city to observe me working, and I received my student teaching credit. I spent six weeks with one excellent teacher, and another six weeks with a real witch. Afterward, I was given my own first grade class.

The witch was one of those duplicitous teachers we all remember from our childhood or children's horror movie. She had managed to make herself the darling of the P.T.A., and everyone thought she was a fine, experienced teacher. She surely was experienced in manipulating people's opinion and being so seemingly fond of children. I did not know how very bad she was until I took a third grade class the following year. My students, who had been in her first grade class, told me horror stories about how she handled discipline in their class. Mrs. C., a tiny lady with large breasts and who always teetered on high heel shoes, had the habit of putting incorrigible first graders into her teachers closet. In this school, and in those days, the teachers had a built-in closet that was quite large. Now we have only tiny cupboard spaces to hold only a coat and purse, and it needs to have a lock. These new closets would not even hold a first grader. Mrs. C. would also put bad children under her desk, a rather small place next to her high heels and angry feet. The children did not like her much and even feared her. But the mothers that were active in the rather small P.T.A. could be assured that their children received better treatment.

One day, while my third graders were at P.E. class, I walked passed Mrs. C. standing right outside her classroom door, her back flat against the wall. I smiled and asked what she was doing. Her index finger went to her lips as she said, "Shh, they don't know I'm out here. I'm checking to see how they behave when I am not in the room." I asked if she didn't think they were aware of her being there. She thought they did not. The truth was that when Mrs. C. was out of the building, with illness, conferences, and such, these kids were difficult for the substitute teacher. I'm certain that they knew she was waiting to pounce on them suddenly, catching them at whatever kids can find to do. In preparation for a "back to school night" Mrs. C. had her students draw an outline of themselves, their total body, and then color it in to look like themselves. It was not great art. Probably the only resemblance to the student was the color and length of hair and the eye colors. These were drawn on large butcher paper that all schools had on large rolls. These paper "puppets" were set in an upright position (a stick glued along the torso) in each child's chair. I could not help thinking that there was not much difference between the paper children and the subdued and overly controlled students, who sat obediently in those same chairs, with about the same amount of movement, as when Mrs. C. was there in charge. For years, I always told everyone that I kept teaching each year so that at least thirty children would not have a Mrs. C.

Teaching was very gratifying, much to my surprise. I had thought from the college preparation that it would be very trying and quite boring. What a great mistake! Teaching was interesting; new children each year, and every day was so entertaining. I loved working with the kids. I taught first grade one year and then grade three for two years in this wonderful district. I am so sorry that new teachers coming in will not have the great experiences that I had, as the times and techniques have changed so that teachers are not allowed to be creative or personable with their students. Here are some of my early encounters with great kids.

Interviews

My first year of teaching I had an adorable little boy, Doug. He was bright and learned easily. He was all boy, never a bully, but respected by all his first grade classmates. He was muscular and very athletic, along with being good academically. Doug was also quite physically attractive. He had curly light brown hair that he tossed with dramatic head flicks, and he walked with a rather adult swagger. The classmates all were impressed with Doug. In those early days teachers had to be on the playground at lunch and recess. We had no "aides" or "paras". Whenever it was my turn outside, Doug always walked with me. He talked a lot about his dad and never mentioned his mother. One day he began complaining about his dad. "I don't know why my dad never remarried, other guys do." I was unaware that he was without his mother. I did not ask him about what had happened to her, believing he would provide that information if and when he wished. I did start paying more attention to him as I thought he was deprived of motherly concern. He continued talking to me about his dad and praising him in all areas. He asked if I had children, at this time I did not. Parent teacher conferences were coming and I was interested in meeting Doug's father and finding out more information. Doug gave the impression that he was interviewing for a new mother. I had told him I was married, but he continued his discussions about how he was so sorry his dad never married and how nice I was. On the night of conferences Doug's dad *and* his mother showed up to discuss Doug. My little friend seemed very uncomfortable and embarrassed. The next day I asked him why he had told me he had no mother. His response was that he liked me and thought I would be a good mom. I have no idea how he planned to change things, but I was very flattered.

O.K.

When I was a beginning teacher there were few "special education classes". I suppose that many severely retarded children were either home-schooled or put in an institution. Teresa was retarded. She had Downs Syndrome and her I.Q. was only in the high 50's. She was repeating grade one for the second time in a regular classroom, at her parents' request. She was small for her age and so did not seem out of place, and all of her classmates loved her. She had learned to count to ten, knew some of her letters, and made a capital "T" for her name. Her concerned teachers had given her as much attention as they could and had helped her to gain these few skills. I was new in the building and had a grade one classroom although Teresa was not my student.

One very troublesome day when it seemed nothing was going well, I ran into a couple of first grade students in the hallway near the girls' restroom. "Help! Teresa has locked all the stall doors and we can't get in!" complained one little girl. I hastily opened the restroom door just as Teresa was starting out. She had locked each stall on the inside, and then crawled under the doors and left the stalls locked. Being frustrated and hurried I said, "Teresa, you go back in there and unlock all those doors, right now!" She looked up at me angrily and placed her little hands on her hips, and with her chin and lower lip out she said fiercely, "No, Ancer". I did not realize that she knew my name—even though she could not correctly pronounce it. I was stunned. This child did not hurry to follow my orders and she was so defiant. I suddenly realized this was a very poor approach to getting compliant behavior. I took a deep breath, put my arm around Teresa's shoulder, and calmly said. "Look, Teresa, the doors are all locked in here and the girls can't get in to use the bathroom. Would you do me a big favor and crawl under the doors and unlock them for me? I am too big to do that."

"O.K. Ancer", she said with a big smile, and promptly crawled under each stall door and opened them for the other girls. I was surprised at how a distinct change in my attitude and behavior had promoted such a great response. This was a great learning moment for the teacher on how to approach children, not just "special" students but all kids. Love and understanding was such a better alternative to dictatorial demands.

If She Says So

A few years later, while teaching third grade, it was my pleasure to have a feisty redheaded boy named Ronnie. Ronnie was more than out going. He ran everything. One day when I asked the class to settle down and stop talking so that I could resume some instruction, he announced,

"Any of you who don't will deal with ME!" I let Ronnie know that I could handle it and went on with class.

A conversation with the teachers in the lounge, including the principal, revealed that one fourth grade teacher was having discipline problems with a student. She said, "What do you do when a child thinks he can take over the classroom?" I responded rather sarcastically, "Just let him take something down the hallway." The principal with whom I was in full accord, and who knew Ronnie well, jokingly said, "Oh Mrs. Lancer, are you saying that Ronnie has taken over your classroom, and that is why he is in the hall all the time?" We had discussed Ronnie, lovingly, on many occasions, and he knew that part of my way of handling Ronnie's ADHD was to let him run an errand when his "inside activity" grew too strong. The principal had been the recipient of a number of unnecessary notes that I felt Ronnie needed to walk all the way down two long hallways to deliver at the office. Over several years this principal had assigned numerous students with behavioral problems to my class, as he approved of my methods of handling them. The teacher group realized this was friendly joshing from a very savvy principal. These were the days before Ritalin and other drugs were prescribed to kids, even before the ADHD diagnoses were made.

Ronnie was a very nice asset to the classroom. He made things interesting and all the kids loved him. When we were about to have field days, (This used to be a competition for athletic events for the school—now it is no longer competitive as everyone gets a ribbon just for participation) Ronnie was expecting to do well as he was very good at physical activities. He ran faster than most of the other boys, even though his legs appeared to go in a circle like an eggbeater. His speed was such that even with the extra, ineffective movements he could still outrun his competition. I had spent time on the playground with my class giving them extra help and suggestions for the running and jumping events. Ronnie was more than ready, and he won all ribbons in the races he entered. Our class was proud of him. He was a hero.

One day, Ronnie asked me during class time how old I was. Thinking that he would know it was an inappropriate question, I jokingly answered, "Eighteen".

"Eighteen?" questioned Ronnie.

"Well," I said smiling, feeling sure that he knew that age was ridiculous, "Maybe eighteen and a half".

The class all giggled and I assumed that they appreciated the joke. Some days later I needed to call in for a sick day. On my return to school after a one day absence, I asked the kids how the day had gone with the substitute. They reported that everything was alright. Then one girl said, "Except Ronnie got in trouble with the substitute and had to go to the office." I was comforted in the fact that the principal was well acquainted with Ronnie, and I knew that the punishment had been justly handled. I asked the group what Ronnie had done. It seems that the substitute teacher, for some unknown and strange reason, had asked the group how old their regular teacher was. When Ronnie told her I was eighteen and the class had laughed, the substitute said,

"No teacher is eighteen".

Ronnie in anger responded, "If she says she is eighteen, then she is eighteen".

The resultant anger on both sides caused enough conflict that Ronnie ended up with the principal. I did explain to Ronnie that I was only joking, and apologized for not making it clear to him that it was not my accurate age. I told him ages of students graduating from high school, and that there was then another three or four years of college, and that was why the sub did not believe him. I let him know it was all my fault and that I did not mean to get him in trouble. I have not lied to the children again about my age, that is until I was about to retire, then I was telling them that I was one hundred, and then, I did make sure that they knew it was a joke.

Sally's Keeper

After several years of teaching grade three, I was feeling quite confident that I knew how classroom dynamics worked for that age. I was able to instill social attitudes into the students. I was a good motivator for correct behavior and taught understanding and acceptance for each child. We had a very positive atmosphere in the room and most of the children were happy, and all were part of the group.

I had a morning when I received an important phone call just as the starting bell rang. The principal had asked me to stay in the office and take the call. I assumed that he would have another teacher bring my class into the school and get them settled, or that he would do that for me. I finished the call and hurried on down the two long hallways to my room. The children were all in their seats, except for my first reading group, which had brought their chairs and made their circle in the front of the classroom. The room was still and one of the members of the reading group was introducing the new vocabulary words to the group. She even had my lesson plan book opened to the day's work. The students at their desks were quiet, and had started some seat-work that this very responsible girl had given the class. I asked who had brought them in and the answer was that the teacher in the next room had just told them to go on in and take their seats. She did not watch to see how they performed. They had put their bags, coats, and other things away, and taken their seats on their own. The lovely girl who took over was one of my brighter and more motivated students, and I was very pleased that the children were all being cooperative and helpful. They said that they had wanted to surprise me, and they surely did. I don't believe I ever was in a class, when I was a student in school, where this could have happened.

The class was so well integrated and well behaved, everyone was respectful of all the other's strengths and shortcomings. Even David was well accepted. David was one of those kids who easily trips, makes social blunders, and is not very good at interacting with peers. He had a history of being very distracted and disturbing others during class. I was aware that the principal had placed him in my room because he felt good about my classroom teaching and student management. David was a boy who had been discussed in the teachers' lounge for several years. His prior teachers had all been at their wits end about how to cope with him. David's parents had spent a lot of time at school discussing ways to help with David's problems. I was feeling disgustingly proud of myself about how well David was integrated into our classroom, and how well accepted he was by his peers. Still, he had behaviors that we ignored, helped him to change, or just accepted as "being David".

I had a teenage cousin who decided that I should have a living mascot as a classroom addition. My cousin was always catching toads and other critters. He had been to the local canal and seen a number of salamanders. He suggested that my third graders would enjoy having one at school as they were easy to care for and interesting to watch. I agreed, not being familiar with salamanders. I did not foresee the smell or the constant cleaning of the makeshift aquarium. I grew tired quite quickly of "Sally Salamander" and her stench. The children still loved Sally although she was not as interesting as she initially had been. We had a schedule and children were still eager to sign up to change Sally's water and to feed her. When it came time to have the Christmas break we discussed the fact that Sally could not be left unattended at the school for the two week period. Of course, many of the children begged to be the one who could take Sally to their home and care for her. David was one that eagerly asked to be chosen for this wonderful experience. I stupidly (yet, I assumed, *wisely*) thought that David would be a good choice for the job. I gleefully suspected that Sally would not return from the break if she were put in David's care. My decision, I remarkably told myself, was to allow David to have a special recognition and a special job to increase his standing in the group. How very self-serving of me! Did I not foresee how angry the class would be when David would have the blame for our loss of beloved Sally?

When we reconvened in January, David came up to my desk and said, "Something awful happened to Sally." Of course, I thought to myself, this is what we expected. Sally needed her water changed. David didn't mean to turn on the hot water—at least not *that* hot. "It was scary", he continued, "She just shriveled all up. I'm sorry". David did seem sorry. I certainly had no sad feelings as I really didn't want Sally back. I was somewhat surprised at the class reaction. Initially they were upset with David, but not terribly. I wondered if they had tired of her smell and lacked interest in her rather boring personality. I did tell the class it was more my fault than David's (boy, was this true!). I said that I had not gone over Sally's care with him, and that I should have talked with his mother about how to change her water, feed her, etc. The class obediently became protective of David and let him know he was forgiven for the loss of Sally. With more teaching experience and understanding that I gained later, had I seen this kind of decision, that reflected negatively upon a student made by another teacher, I would have been thoroughly disgusted. I still have guilt about poor David.

The next year the college classes I took were instruction in teaching "emotionally disturbed children". My principal was somewhat amused. "Why do you suppose," he said smiling, "That every teacher with whom I have placed David has taken courses on the emotionally disturbed child after their experience?" There are not too many Davids but it is a good thing for the teachers to have these courses. Maybe they will not send the classroom pet home with the wrong kid.

Chapter Two

HISTORY OF THE SPECIAL PROGRAMS

I began teaching in the late fifties and taught for forty-some years. I taught for three years in a very education-friendly and teacher-friendly district under a superintendent who was the model of a great man, educator, and humanist. He and his wife had a handicapped child that was severely impaired. The child had hydrocephalus, more commonly termed "water-head" at that time. Presently we have a surgical cure for this condition. A shunt is placed in the head to direct the fluid, that is building in the brain, back down into the stomach area for absorption. At the time that this child was born there was no treatment and the child would often die shortly after birth. Some individuals lived for longer periods if the fluid build-up developed more slowly. This child lived into his twenties, and the parents remodeled the basement to accommodate all his needs. His head was so enlarged that he was in a wheelchair for the support of the weight, and the basement had ramps and large spaces for his wheelchair mobility. The parents, rather than institutionalize their son, kept him at home and cared for him themselves—with some support for breaks away from the care. He was in their home until his death in his early twenties. The superintendent must have learned from his own trials as he was extremely compassionate for all the special cases in his district. That district became a model for the treatment of special education students. This superintendent deservedly has a high school named for him.

After the three years of teaching in a fantastic setting, I moved to another suburb of the nearby large city. I had two years of being a stay-at-home mom,and then returned to teaching. The new district that I worked in was not very large at the time (early sixties). There was only one high school and two junior high schools, and under ten grade schools. At the time I am writing this, 2011, there are currently five high schools, seven middle-schools (now grades 6-8, before it was junior high, grades 6-9) and about twenty grade schools. The suburban sprawl has enlarged the small city (that used to be a little more than just a suburb) enough that it is now one of the larger cities in the state.

"Special Education" in this district, in the sixties, consisted of several classrooms of "retarded students", with only two teachers at the elementary level, one at junior high and one at the high school level. Shortly after I began teaching, the district placed a classroom of "disturbed children" in one of the elementary schools. The idea was to intervene with the severe behavioral problems in the child's early years and rehabilitate these students to enable them to reenter the regular classroom. An older teacher with experience in special eduction taught this class for the first two years. I was teaching in regular grade three. I became interested in behavioral disorders and took some classes for preparation in special education for the emotionally disturbed. The teacher who began the "emotionally disturbed" classroom was quickly burned out and left the district. I was given this classroom its third year with my minimal preparation. I was working on a masters degree in special education and then went on to earn a doctorate in higher education and psychology. At the time that I started working with the "emotionally disturbed" classroom the new interest in specific "learning disabilities" was becoming prevalent. A classroom was housed with both special student identifications for two years and then the students were split into two categories. I opted to teach the "emotionally disturbed", and a teacher who had earlier worked with the "retarded" program was assigned to the "learning disabilities" group. She took additional classes to learn about this new area. In these early years, our school district employed one psychologist, one social worker and a few speech therapists, several teachers for retardation, and we two teachers for "L.D." and "emotionally disturbed".

The state and federal governments were highly involved in the guidelines for student inclusion in these programs, as funds from both state and federal coffers were being used. I continued my classes in this area in both evenings and summers. My classroom was under the guidance of the county psychiatrist in charge of mental health services. The parents of my students met weekly with a social worker from the county mental health association, the principal, and myself. As time progressed, several other classrooms for special education evolved from growth of the district, and new findings in the field of special education.

After my five years with this program for the emotionally disturbed, I left to study for my doctorate at the university, where I was a graduate assistant with a research assistance-ship and a sabbatical leave from my school district. While there, I instructed teachers in the diagnosis and remediation of learning disabilities. I also taught introduction to special education, and also student teaching seminars. When I returned to teaching in this same school district, the special education program was extending rapidly. There was national interest in the field of learning disabilities and the colleges and universities were graduating many specialists in this field along with other specific areas, such as autism, emotionally disturbed, hearing handicapped, and others. In my district there were now two classes of emotionally disturbed students, and more speech therapists, teachers of hearing impaired, and visual disabilities. There were also a number of new teachers being hired to work with learning disabilities, and I went into this area of instruction. The district now had two high schools, four middle schools and a number of new elementary schools. The district was growing extensively.

Because of the specific guidelines for "staffing" students for the assistance in special education programs mandated by the federal and state governments—and because of the funding from these government agencies—the district set up a rather impressive "permanent staffing team". On this team there were several elementary principals, the district psychologist, the district social worker, the director of special services, the specialists involved in the student's testing, the regular classroom teacher, and finally, the parents of the child being discussed. These "staffings" consisted of reports given of the functioning level of the student in his academic skills, the tests administered by any specialists involved, followed by a discussion to determine eligibility in any specific programs. As time progressed and there were more and more staffings, the "permanent" team was disbanded and these staffings were no longer held in the administration board room, but in each individual school where the child attended. The district now had a number of psychologists, more social workers, and increasingly more special education teachers in various areas of expertise. Now, some thirty years later, things have reverted back to fewer procedures much as before the influx of information, training, and government control of the special education field. At this point the school identifies the children to receive services at each elementary school. The school is told the number of children that they should select for help depending upon statistics of enrollment and incidence of "disabilities". There are no massive staffings and the special education teachers are classified as servers of mild, moderate or severe disabilities, rather than teachers of each specific disability. The severe cases are in self-contained classrooms, but the mild and moderate services are for any disabilities, and the teachers instruct all areas of disabilities either in a small classroom, or right in the regular classroom during regular class periods.

Chapter Three

THE EARLY PROGRAM FOR THE EMOTIONALLY DISTURBED

After teaching three years with the regular classroom students, in my second district of employment, I began working with the "emotionally disturbed" students. My principal recommended me for the only classroom of this type in my district. I had begun taking classes to gain this certification and, as it was a new field, no one else was close to certification. There had been a teacher for this class in its first and second years of operation. After working a short while with the students I was made aware that the teacher, now retired, had spent most of the school-day having the class watch the learning channels on the television. I rather imagine that not much learning had taken place. The group was initially made up of six boys and several others were added as the year progressed. We were housed in a regular school room. At that time, I was rather short and also slightly built and several of the boys were much taller than I. There was a very nice sixth grade teacher in the next room who was very helpful. He had been there in the school, and in the room next to the class the year before, and so he offered that, if at any time there was a problem that I could not handle, he was there to be of assistance.

In the college classes that I had taken in this subject area, it was stated that the best way to staff these programs was with two adults, a man and a woman. This was to give the students sexual role models, and also for disciplinarian reasons. When there was "acting out" one teacher could remove a child while the other continued the class. I mentioned this to the director of the program for the district. He did not seem impressed. Jim, my helpful neighbor, was called upon a few times to watch my class for a moment or two while I conferred outside (we had doors to the outside for each classroom.) with the student to solve their current distress.

The next year the district added another teacher and another classroom. My new co-worker Jan had seven boys and I also had seven. I moved to the next building where the third grade classrooms were housed. This next year our room had another classroom next door that was separated by a folding wall. These were the days when teachers took turns going out on playground duty or to duty in the lunchroom. I was always concerned because the other teachers did not appreciate my boys being outside with the other students, as they tended to get into trouble. I often went out, even when it was not my turn, just to monitor my boys. Jan, of course, had the same problem.

The teacher behind our folding wall was very interested in our class. She was near retirement and was old and heavy. It was hard for her to get around on the playground especially when we had snow. She had grade three but the principal had given her a very small class of only fifteen students. The administration was trying to get rid of her; it took another year and assigning her to a new school way out in the boondocks, with mud and no parking, to accomplish that task. Meanwhile, she was so concerned about what we were doing that she followed the boys about the playground when it was her assignment to monitor the students outside. She would complain about them to me, so I asked the boys to please stay far away from her on the playground. They said they could not as she followed them everywhere. I looked out the windows a few times and did, in fact, see her hobbling about behind them. On a number of occasions I noticed that the folding "wall" was unlatched and opened a few inches. I continued to scold the class and ask them not to unlatch the wall. They finally told me that it was Miss A., that she was trying to spy on them. I did not really believe them until one day when she stopped me in the morning and asked, "How crazy are they? What kinds of things do they do?" The boys themselves had said "She wants to know how crazy we are"

The next year I was moved to a storage closet for audio-visual equipment. The room was in the hallway. It was larger than a usual closet, but with a rippled glass wall its entire length. It was right across from the boys restroom and so the traffic was distracting. Also distracting was the visual disturbance of the rippled glass all across the front of the room, as the boys could see distorted images of people passing in the hallway. Children often put their faces to the windows trying to look in. I had several very hyperactive boys for whom I had gotten carrels. The carrels were hastily constructed plywood dividers made by carpenters in the school district. They had a shelf area for a desk and had three sides to make the work area private, so the boys would not distract each other. They used the regular school chairs to sit on in their enclosed areas. We pretended that the boys had "offices" and I gave them "coffee breaks", and we had play phones from which they received pretend calls. Regular classrooms had drinking fountains and sinks. If we needed water, I had to line the boys up and walk them to the adjoining building where there was a fountain. Once a week I would give them an art lesson with Jan's class, in her room where we had a sink.

The following year, the district made the decision to follow the state guidelines and have the class staffed by a man and a woman. They added "Crazy John" as a team teacher, whom I believe was in more emotional trouble than any of our students. He came from a large, very religious family and told wild tales. One of my favorites was of how his father threw a pitchfork into the utter of a very full milking cow. He did many things that were distressing to me. We were restricted from meeting alone with any of the administrators of the program, the main one being a psychiatrist in charge of the county mental health. John and I were also staffed with a social worker, also not too well adjusted, who scheduled regular counseling session with, the now, six boys in the program. We were assigned several classrooms in the Sunday school section of a nearby Methodist church, from whom the school district contracted the space. We could also make use of the gymnasium where John would toss baskets with the boys. Had we each taken two children apiece and worked with them, I believe the results would have been better.

The social worker was a tiny lady in her sixties with died blonde hair and she was very feminine. She would sit on top of the desks and swing her legs like a little girl, when talking to me and John. She had regular sessions with each child and all three of us discussed their therapy with the director, the psychiatrist in charge. John and I were both concerned about the capabilities of this strange little lady. The boys did not seem to relate well with her. The psychiatrist in charge was very confident of her training. Once, when John and I saw some inappropriate interaction with one of the students, we were discussing how we felt she was not very adept at "reaching" her clients, John surprised me with a proposition about her. He said, "She is very fragile and we could break her if we worked on it." I was horrified. What did he think he could do? I had been concerned about the way that he treated the boys from time to time. He would often provoke them to anger and then seem pleased that they were out of control. I talked to him about this and he only responded that he liked to get them "riled up" as then they would come out with what was important in their therapy. He had come from a job situation in a hospital setting. I told him that this might be a valid approach in an institutional setting, but that we were trying to get the boys to learn to control themselves and reenter a regular classroom setting.

Over the following weeks, I watched John being passive aggressive in his continual attacks to make our social worker feel inadequate. I could not report my concerns to anyone because of the agreement that none of us could speak without it being in a total group session. It was distressing to watch, even though I did not think the social worker was doing a good job. Finally, as we neared the end of the school year, the social worker had a "nervous breakdown". I don't know how much of John's efforts and how much of her own personal situation caused this; but, I felt very sorry for her, and somewhat fearful of John.

When we were housed in the church building, John and I separated the six boys into two groups of three each. John took one group for math and science instruction, and I took the other for reading and language, then we would exchange students to deliver instruction to the other three students. We both taught our groups in the same classroom using opposite ends of the room to keep the students' focus on one instructor. One morning I heard John laughing with Bill, a very tall fifth grader who was a very nervous and easily agitated young man. I listened to Bill tell John how upset and worried he was about what he had done the previous night. He had taken his flashlight and flashed it at a plane that was near and approaching landing. We were near a large metropolitan airport. Bill expressed the concern that he was in real trouble and would possibly be arrested for trying to divert the plane and potentially causing it to crash. John agreed with Bill that it was a very frightening thing that he had done. I waited to hear John tell him that a flashlight was very small compared to the landing lights, and that it was probably completely unnoticed. Instead, John continued feeding Bill's fears, and said that perhaps they would be checking on the area where the light was, and finally identify Bill. I was horrified as I heard Bill's fears escalating. When we exchanged our students for the next instruction time, I had Bill in my group. I spent quite a while trying to undo what John had done. I reassured Bill that the landing field and lights far outshone the small light from a flashlight. I described intensity of both, and the length and amount of light that was part of the landing field. He finally agreed that his actions could not have caused any difficulty for the pilot. Later, I asked John why he played into Bill's anxieties. He just laughed and said he liked to see Bill "all upset".

Another time John was throwing baskets with the boys in the gymnasium while I looked on. He was saying things to Bill that I could not hear. I noticed Bill becoming somewhat agitated. Suddenly Bill started yelling and crying, and ran off the court. John took him down the hall to see the social worker. When I asked him later what had happened, he admitted that he had provoked Bill on purpose as he would then "come out with things that were meaningful". I again stated my disapproval of these methods in our setting. He dismissed the topic with a statement that he had seen this process work. I felt that John was antagonistic toward the students, and had no real concern for their improvement.

The next year, the school district had completed a facility for our program on the grounds of another elementary school. John, the social worker, and I had been asked to give our input into how to build the classroom. The building was funded with a government grant. It housed several offices for the county mental health specialists, our classroom, two restrooms—one was for the kids and one for the adults—and an office and reception area. The space was used for county counseling and our class. Our classroom had high windows, storage space for materials and toys, and an observation room with a one way window. Again, we had only six students to start, several more were added later. We then had our first girl student! She was a terror. The students took lunch with the regular classroom students in the adjoining elementary school. They also had time on the playground with the regular students if their behavioral skills warranted it. We had a newly hired social worker assigned to therapy for the class. I was still concerned about teaching with John.

The problem for me in this last setting, besides John, was working with the mental health personnel that were housed in our building. We had a lot of social contact with them and I was amazed at how maladjusted folks in the psychology field appeared to be. We would, when the school was not in session, when the children in our group were not attending for some reason, or on a lunch period, accompany some of the therapists, secretary, and the county psychiatrists to a restaurant for lunch. The chief psychiatrist was the most difficult. He often made very Freudian comments about everything. Once he mentioned to me that possibly I was uncomfortable with the knife at my place setting. When I made no response, he pointed out several more phallic symbols. I finally told him that what made me uncomfortable was his continually focusing on the psychiatric jargon. I asked if we couldn't discuss some current events, weather, or the like.

The secretary was a sweet, unaffected young lady who was quite naive. She had given notice that she would be leaving in a month or so. The head psychiatrist said that he was going to give all applicants a Rorschach test. I replied that I thought this was unnecessary and even ridiculous, and questioned the purpose. He responded that he liked to know all about the people with whom he worked, all their "inner thoughts and weaknesses".

Just a few weeks later, when we were all at lunch, he questioned the sweet secretary about her sexual experience before her marriage. He accompanied the question with the comment that he had enjoyed numerous sexual experiences with others beside his wife, and that he was very *comfortable* in relating this. The poor unsuspecting secretary responded that she had not had any other experiences other than her husband. She then proudly stated, "I am comfortable in telling that." He turned to me, the only other female in the group, and asked about my experience. I responded, "This is a very personal topic that I'm not sure we should be discussing, and I am comfortable in saying it is really no one's business other than mine." I thought this would stop some of his continual psychiatric prodding. I was mistaken, as he continually indulged in this kind of communication with the group.

At Christmas time, John and I were invited to the county mental health services party. The group in our building was a small part of the total employees. We were told that there was a gift exchange. The "head man" proposed that if we did not know the person whose name we had drawn, he could fill us in on the personality of that person to help us select a gift. He gave examples of gifts given in the past. They were mostly joke gifts focused on the insecurities or personality problems of the recipient. He said that one therapist, that had a "mother fixation", was given a nursing bottle. He suggested several other demeaning gifts. I bought some cotton gloves and made puppets on the fingers. I felt that this applied to the profession without being personally insulting. The party was on a Friday night. Those in our building began some festive alcohol consumption early in the day. I'm sure the school district would have been upset with the alcohol on the premises, as it was against district policy and this was a district building. By the time the party started there was already some drunkenness. John and I were invited to go with the "head man" in his car. He offered to drive to the party at the county office and then drive us back to the school. I endured a number of psychiatric jokes on the way, and a lot of "in house" humor at the party. There were the usual insulting gifts exchanged. On the return to the school, another psychologist accompanied us in the car. He had been drinking rather heavily and was saying things that concerned our "head man". One thing I remember was that he told everyone that he was giving therapy to an airline pilot who was having multiple affairs with a number of different stewardesses—with whom he was also consulting He said for time reasons he was cutting some of his clients. He said he would cut the stewardesses, they hadn't the money anyway, but that he wanted to keep the pilot as he would like to "find out how he can do it".

After this year, with lots of interaction with the psychiatric community, I spent a year on a sabbatical leave working on my doctorate at the university. Upon my return, I taught corrective reading, took another year leave for my doctorate, and returned to the school district. Because of my problems with John, who was still in the district, and my negative experiences with the mental health personnel, I decided to teach the "learning disabled" instead of returning to the psychological invironment.

Chapter Four

MY CLASSROOMS OF EMOTIONALLY DISTURBED

When I started with the program, there were already six boys assigned to the classroom. They had been instructed the prior year by a teacher no longer in the district. The classroom was in a fairly new school building (grades kindergarten through sixth) that architects had convinced the district to build. The plan was a three wing structure with walkways between the wings. This was a "California Style" architectural model that was being put in a western state with heavy snow seasons. The walkways were open, making it necessary many times in the school year, to have the students put on winter outer wear to cross to another wing. The cafeteria, offices, gym, library, music room, and teachers' lounge were all in a center wing. The early grades, kindergarten through third were in the west wing. The grades four through six were in the east wing. My class was in the east wing. There were drinking fountains and sinks in each full sized classroom. There was a girls' restroom and a boys' restroom in both the east and west wings. The faculty rest room was in the center wing. It was necessary to line my group up and lead them to lunch or to any special programs that were usually given in the gym. The classrooms themselves were structured in this new, modern way that precluded any doorways between class rooms. My door and the adjoining classroom door were about two feet apart in the hallway. If a teacher were instructing in the front of each of these classrooms, they would be talking at cross purposes. Luckily, Jim did not do loud instruction at the front of his room, and I did instruction throughout my room. In the west wing, where the younger classes met, the classrooms had folding walls, in order to open several rooms into a larger room. In the many years since this ill-conceived school was built, the district has found it more practical to enclose the walkways from the weather, put doors on the classrooms, and build sturdy walls to replace the folding ones.

My room had an outside door with a small cement slab adjoined. This is where I could take my students for private counseling, or to calm emotional outbursts as needed. My friend Jim, in the adjoining class, had offered to "keep an eye on the group" if needed. I did need help frequently

My room was furnished with my desk, numerous student desks, a sand table (left from the prior teacher), and a circular table for group instruction. Three of the boys, ages seven to twelve, were close to being non-readers, they were reading at only a pre-primer level, being able to decode only twenty five to fifty words. One boy was reading at second grade level. Two, who had more behavioral problems than academic, were sixth grade students reading at fifth grade level.

I used regular math workbooks on the appropriate level for each of the boys. There were reading workbooks that accompanied the readers so that they could have reading materials at their level. I had spelling lists for their grade level, they all wrote in their diaries or journals daily for language instruction. Science was addressed through a twice a week television program on the educational channel. As the boys' behavior improved they were allowed to go into science and social study sessions in regular classrooms for their appropriate age. The boys were also given regular P.E. and music classes with their age groups as their behavior warranted.

We started the day with a share time which developed into a "show-and-tell" in a rather short time. We then had writing and spelling practice. With only six boys, I was able to give them individual help and instruction as needed. Then came math, and I made worksheets or used workbook pages appropriate to their level of understanding. We had snack breaks daily with milk and crackers. On a rare occasion a child would be excluded from snack break for severe infringement of classroom rules or very disruptive behavior. There was a break time in the afternoon for play at the sand table. As the boys improved in overall behaviors, the students were able to participate in the total school's recess period. on the playground. At the beginning of the year, I needed to be with the boys at lunch time in the cafeteria and often spent some of lunch recess on the playground with them. Later in the year they were able to tolerate playground time without me. I was then scheduled with the other teachers for playground, lunch and recess duties.

It may sound as if the day were orderly and manageable, but initially the behaviors were terrible. The boys would often have an outbreak of anger, and be very disruptive. Peter, Steven, and Bobby were eleven and twelve years old, and very strong. I was lucky to be able to usually have just one boy out of control at a time. There were only a few occasions in which it was necessary to call upon the principal for help with severe behaviors. Early in the year there were times when a boy might climb up on his desk, the sand table, or the counter. There were often loud bursts of temper, tears, and often refusals to attend to work. By the spring, the boys had developed enough self control and favorable interactions that the class mostly ran very smoothly. As an example; one day my close teacher friend, a teacher in grade two, asked if I would take her student, John, in my room the following morning. John was a real problem in her class and with his bad behavior could easily be seen as a future candidate for my program. Sindy, my friend and John's second grade teacher, was having a parent visitation for the entire morning. She was more than concerned about how John would make the entire class seem poorly run. I agreed to take him, but when I told the boys about the arrangement, warning them so it would not be a surprise, they were very upset. One of them said, "We don't want John in our class. Everyone will think *we* are crazy like John". John's reputation was throughout the school. John did "visit". The boys were supportive and showed him how nicely they could behave. He was rather quiet and intimidated by the older boys.

We had only one outburst from John and it was at the beginning of the day. The boys were now priding themselves with the results of their improved behaviors, and several teachers had remarked at how well the boys behaved.

In the spring there were several other students added to our classroom. Initially there was some regressive behavior from the original group in reaction to adjusting to new personalities in the class. The more normal behaviors, developed over the months, were very helpful in the indoctrination of new students who needed to follow class rules and behaviors. It usually took several weeks for the new student to adjust, and for the class to assimilate a new person in the group.

The school district had just begun an innovative reading program based on a phonetic approach. It was called "Words In Color". The phonetic sounds were given varying colors and there were numerous charts on which colored words were printed. The teachers were trained in the special instruction. The district held training sessions before school began. The program was specific to grades one through three, as the older children were considered to be reading already. The teacher used the charts and a pointer to "dictate" the reading to the children, who sat in small groups and responded orally. My boys demonstrated interest and it turned out to be a very good approach for them. This program, as other innovative instruction has done, lasted only a few short years. The program was designed to teach adults who were foreign speaking to learn English. Many of the phonetic examples on the charts were inappropriate for young children, such as "pneumatic" and "rhododendron". I have since used the charts and books to teach high school non-readers, ESL adult students, and older children that I was home tutoring. I found it very useful.

The county mental health facilities were employed to assist and advise for this special education program. We had weekly meetings with parents, the principal, the mental health social worker, and myself. At this meeting, the designation of disability for the members of the class was discussed. Nationally, in the education field, there was great interest in the new field of "learning disabilities" and associated "brain injury" (no matter how small) that may have impacted a child's learning. There was a national movement to take a child with brain injury through the early physical developmental period. There was a theory that the child had not gone through the expected and natural sequence of physical development, which according to theorist, caused inability to acquire academics. In discussing the problems of the students, the parents discussed whether their child was afflicted with emotional disturbance, or if there had been an incident of brain injury, possibly even with just a difficult birth. It was apparent that the parents took the discussions home, as the boys began to label one another at school. The distinction was difficult to make except in more defining cases such as a known handicapping condition, as Ray had. The boys began calling each other by one of the labels in anger or competitive situations. When I talked with them and let them know this was inappropriate, the boys quit saying anything, but would instead make a sign with their hands indicating "brain injured". The sign was the hand with index and middle fingers raised and wiggled as an insect antennae. The social worker was amused but concerned about the emotional consequences for the boys. He brought up the problem at a weekly parent meeting, asking me which disability was the boys' preferred one for the week. A talk with the parents on the labeling, and my work with the boys, and the problem subsided. The following year, a teacher for "learning disabilities" was hired for a separate class. I was asked to separate the boys accordingly. There were, in some cases, no clear divisions. A second new teacher was added for the "behaviorally disturbed" group, as a number of additional students had been identified to be placed in a special class. This group, and my students who returned, were divided according to age. I opted to teach the younger group.

The group consisted of six boys the first year, Bobby, Phillip, Mike, Ray, Steven and Peter. Steven and Bobby were eleven and twelve years old. Steven was almost at grade level academically. Bobby was almost at grade level for math but could only read twenty to thirty words. Peter was ten and was reading at a fifth grade level. Mike was also ten and was at first grade reading level. Phillip was nine and also performing at a first grade level. Ray was seven and had completed grade one and was almost at grade two level for math and reading. Ray was definitely identified with the brain injured. Bobby and Phillip were definitely emotionally disturbed. Peter and Steven were questionable. Mike had a low I.Q. and was considered to be minimally retarded, along with behavioral problems. How could he have a singular label? The defining of "emotionally disturbed" is questionable on its own. The next year, Rene, who had definitely incurred brain injury from his difficult birth, was placed in my room. I believe the placement was because of his severe handicap and my more extensive training in the field. One might also wonder about Phillip and how his odd behaviors had developed at such an early age.

Chapter Five

MY "CRAZY" BOYS

The Bully

In the first group that I taught, while I was working alone, I had Bobby. He was there for his second year. Bobby was the oldest in the group, he was twelve and should have been in grade six. Back in this day, elementary school was from grades kindergarten through sixth grade. In just a few years the district would change it to grades kindergarten through grade five. Bobby was a large and muscular boy. His family lived near the outskirts of the city on a small farm-like acreage with numerous animals. Bobby lived with his parents and a younger brother. Bobby was treated more like an adult and his parents were very protective of the little brother. They seemed very disappointed in Bobby's lack of achievement. He was in the program because of his low academic skills and his disruptive behavior.

One of my methods for gaining production in academic work from my students, who had been failing for a time, was to reward them with "M &M's". Justification for this was psychological studies on reward systems and the fact that edible rewards were the best for initial behavior modification. Because of the age of the subjects and the low level of motivation, it worked beautifully. The tangible and edible rewards were gradually changed to less frequent and finally to intrinsic rewards, as described in the recent literature that I had perused. Initially all the boys looked forward to their rewards. They all seemed to love the chocolate treats and were competitive in the numbers of candies that they were able to gain. They were given certain amounts for completing their various areas of work. Bobby was very diligent. He seemed very proud and waited eagerly for his "M&M's", after my checking his work, or his completing the individual instruction time. One day the boys were moving their desks into a different alignment and Bobby's desk was bumped hard as he pushed it. Out of his desk flew a cardboard carton that had once held cottage cheese. It rolled on the floor and fell open. Out rolled a whole quart of "M&M's". Bobby had been saving his rewards. We were all astonished that there were so many. The boys asked him about it and he seemed embarrassed. I remarked that the candies were his to do with as he pleased, and that the rest of the class had made a decision to eat theirs. Bobby wished to keep them. It seemed as though Bobby might have been ahead in the usual progress of the rewards system.

Bobby had come from a school where he had been given numerous suspensions for his behavior. He often got into fights with others, was seen as a bully, hated school, and was a difficult child to control. He was reading at a pre-primer level and was extremely discouraged. His self esteem was at the bottom because of his poor school achievement. He was larger than any of the other boys, and stronger. This was a perfect place for him to continue his "bullying".

Bobby picked one classmate after another to be the object of his attacks. He was appropriate in the classroom, but on the playground he would single out a student and become physically abusive. The boys would come back to class and tell how Bobby had started a fight with one of them. Of course he would win. I spent much time taking Bobby outside, while Jim kept an eye on my class. We talked and it finally surfaced that Bobby's little brother was teasing and even hitting Bobby frequently. The parents had let Bobby and his brother know that Bobby could not retaliate, so little brother continued hitting Bobby.

I had talked often to Bobby about how the child he was fighting was smaller, younger, and not as strong as he. He was often asked why he was angry at that child. He had no clear answers. Before I was made aware of the little brother problem, I had started talking about Bobby's behavior to the whole class. All the boys were concerned as they might be the next target. I had talked to all of them about bullying, how it was not fair, and how to handle it. There seemed to be no way to stop Bobby.

In my long conversations with Bobby, I proposed to him that he was so angry about his brother, and his inability to hit him back, that he was taking it out on his classmates because his parents could not stop that. He seemed to be listening and trying to understand. The bullying continued.

One day I told Bobby in front of the others that he had been abusive to most of them and that they would not want to be his friend any longer. I suggested to Bobby that it might be a problem if they *all* decided it could not happen anymore and they, as a group, would defend the child he attacked. I watched their reactions and anticipated what would happen.

For several days it seemed likely that the boys would get after Bobby in a group. It was not my week to be on the playground, but I went out hoping to referee when the situation crystallized. It didn't happen and I grew less concerned. Of course, the day that the boys decided to stop Bobby, I was not there. A teacher came into the teachers' lunchroom and announced, "Two of Laurel's kids were in a fight and then a number of them piled on the big boy. He ran off the playground and is gone." The principal called Bobby's mother—he appeared at home about an hour later.

Our program's weekly meeting the county mental health social worker, the school district director, the principal, parents, and myself was the next evening, Bobby's father was there and seemed quite upset. As the meeting got underway, Bobby's father interrupted the usual proceedings, came to the front of the media center, where we met, and leaned upon the small upright piano. "I want to know", he started with a shaky voice, "What kind of a person is teaching these boys". I was terrified. Now I was in great trouble for instigating a fight. He continued, "What kind of person can understand what is going on with these kids, handle their problems, and even teach them. I can't believe what has happened. "My fears mounted. He continued," Last night my son told me what I had been doing wrong. We have had a lot of problems with him. He bullies at school. He can't read. His school work is terrible. He has been upset for years. Yesterday he ran away from school. We talked about it. It seems that his little brother is always bothering him. He has become so angry because we favor his brother and won't let him hit the little one back. He says that is why he picks on the other kids. He said his teacher helped him to understand what his anger is about. Then the kids were all mad at him. He cried for a long time. But we all understand now. I want to thank his teacher. She has to be a special teacher to help our family with this problem. Thank you Mrs. L."

I was so moved and happy for Bobby. After this incident Bobby's behavior began to change. He did eventually stop the bullying. I was always taught that the anger was caused by frustration of not learning. In this case the anger caused the not learning. Bobby began to read and was soon reading at an appropriate level for his age. He was integrated into the regular classroom the following year—in the junior high school.

Military School

Peter was one of the older boys in the first year. He was not terribly behind academically, but had many behavioral problems that needed to be addressed. He was aggressive toward the younger boys and often hit or pushed others, threw books, pencils, paper, etc. on the floor, yelled out at times, and often refused to follow directions. He was refused recesses and play times and even had to miss snack time on occasion. Peter seemed to prefer Steven to play with and they loved having action figures and cars in the sand table. He started the year very upset about his abilities, the special class, and things going on in his family.

Peter brought a surf board to show to the class. He had lived on the coast before his parents were divorced. Peter lived with his mother and stepfather. He talked about his father living in a nearby city about an hour's drive away. He was concerned that he was going to have to go live with his father. I did not notice a lot of loyalty toward either father figure. His biggest concern was about entering fifth grade in the city where his father was. His mother had been telling him that he was going to go to a military academy in that city, and that he would live with his father for a year. The year away was probably because of his difficulties with behaviors, and his placement in our special class. He kept saying, "I have to pass the test to get into the academy".

In art class one day he drew a picture of a man with a sword. He drew guns and bullets. He made angry comments about the "Krauts". He said that they killed relations of his stepfather in Holland. He became quite silly and sounded very angry and focused on violence. He made a remark about "taking someone to the canal to soften them up". Then Steve said, "Let's do it!". After Ray got in trouble for climbing on the playground fence, Ray reported that Peter had told him to climb the fence. Peter excused the incident by saying that he only asked Ray *how* he would do. His behavior was beginning to effect the other students negatively.

One morning he was particularly upset. He did not want to take his spelling test as he just knew he "would flunk it". He started verbally attacking the other students, threw sand on the floor from the sand table, and insisted that Phillip had done it. I had seen Peter do it. He blamed other things on different students and was just terribly out of sorts. Finally he said, "I have to go to Monument to take a test for the academy tomorrow". He was especially sullen and refused to work, until he decided that he wanted to have play time. Then he hurried and completed his math and took his spelling test. He got all the words perfect. I asked him if he didn't believe his mother would be very proud of him. He responded, "She is never proud of me". He continued to talk about the military school and the fact that he had to have an interview and some tests.

Peter brought his real father's military uniform to show the boys. He said his father had gone to a military school. He said that he was going the next day to the interview. He said his brother had skipped school one day, and that he wanted to ditch school but had decided not to do it. I told him that his mother would be proud of him for making that decision. He said, "I told you she is never proud of me—unless I get an A plus, and that would be a miracle." I had some other concerns about Peter's mother as once when the boys were discussing a movie ("Journey to the Bottom of the Sea"), Peter remarked that, "we are not permitted to watch that because my mother gets upset and takes it out on us".

Peter was out for a day to go to the interview at the academy and take tests. On his return to school he was again quite agitated and had problems with the classmates, lying, throwing things, and verbal outbursts. This behavior continued until there was resolution about his placement. He did pass the interview and his academic tests were acceptable. When it was confirmed that he would leave at semester and go stay with his dad and attend the new school, Peter gradually grew more calm and his behavior gradually improved. He grew more comfortable with his friends in our class. Shortly before his transition to the new city and new school he had some regression in his behavior, but he was not nearly as bad as he had been at the beginning of the year. We were all sorry to lose Peter. He had become a pleasant and interesting classmate. He and Steven had become great pals.

Grandmothers

Steven, at the start of the school year, had initially been very focused on getting attention. He had rather strange mannerisms. He would put his head on the floor, throw his arms and legs up over the sides of his desk, climb upon his desk, climb upon the sand table, and once stood on my desk. This got the attention and some small admiration from his classmates, until every one's behavior began to improve. Then the boys seemed to enjoy more subdued times with the class running smoothly. Steven was also very talkative. When a fellow student was to choose a friend to help him, I asked the boys to put their heads down and close their eyes. Steven would not comply and also angrily stated, "don't choose me". Apparently his concern for not being accepted was very strong. Initially, the boys did not like Steven very much as his conversations were often silly or fantastic. He told a story that he had read in his reader and the facts were all distorted or made up. He and Peter were both reading at a grade five level and the two of them began reading together.

Peter's desire to achieve soon wore off on Steven and his approach to schoolwork became more realistic. One day he wore his scout uniform to school and asked if he could lead the Pledge of Allegiance for the class. The approval that he gained seemed to help him on his start to change his behavior. He brought pictures of mammals for the bulletin board and was putting them into place, but began throwing tacks from the corner of the room. He was having a bad day just as everything seemed to be working out for him. He stayed in at lunch time and talked. It seemed that he was upset because it was going to be his birthday, and he had heard about a birthday surprise. He did not know what his mother was planning and was concerned about sharing with his classmates. It seemed that anything unusual would get Steven to revert to his bad behaviors. All went well for a while. After a few months, it seemed odd that this was the same boy who on occasion would shout out, "Oh, shit".

One day, he became very agitated and was again fighting with the others. He got his bike stuck in the mud and came in for help. I sent Peter to help him. When he came back he put his muddy boots into the classroom sink to wash them off. I made him clean the sink. He had difficulty for most of the day. Finally, in the afternoon, he asked if he could have Wednesday off. He said that his grandmother had passed away on Friday, and that the funeral had been Monday. This was Tuesday. He had been absent the day before but had not told us where he had been. At art time he drew a picture of his grandmother's grave. He made a fence around it and angrily declared, "If anyone disturbs it I'll kill them." He asked if all graves were not on a platform. I told him they were all different and it depended on how the family had decided to plan things. He had a hard time with his work, and it got harder for him to behave in the afternoon. We talked and Steven said, "I am just nervous about my grandmother's funeral". He did know *this* time what was causing him such distress. He talked about his other grandmother and said that she had died when he was four. He said, "I sat on her legs and she was crippled. But that is not what killed her." His final thought that he shared for the day was, "I wish I was dead with my grandmother". All children (and adults) have stress, guilt, and anxiety that effect them with death of loved ones. Steven had made great strides in actually being able to identify what was causing his behaviors this time. With some time he regained the growth he had made.

"Say Yeah"

Howard was the very youngest of the boys in my second year of the program, after we divided the potential students and Jan took her class. Howard was only seven, tall for his age and rather lanky. The first thing you would have noticed about him was his eyeglasses. They were very thick, making it difficult to make eye contact with him, partly because of the thick lenses, and partly because he did not look at you. Howard was very quiet and hardly said a word. His thick wavy hair often hung down on his forehead, he kept his head lowered, and he never looked right at the person talking to him. He seemed rather shy and unobtrusive. However, Howard was a great surprise!

The other boys began to complain about Howard. They said he was calling them names. I was unaware that Howard even communicated with them. He was so quiet in class and never said much. After several complaints from each of the students, I asked what it was that he was saying. "He is calling us all 'Basters'", said one of the boys. I did counsel Howard about name calling, and was somewhat amused by the fact that neither Howard nor the boys seemed to know the correct inflammatory word. The name calling subsided, but other negative behaviors followed it.

Howard was in the class when we were housed in the visual equipment closet, that had the wavy glass panels comprising the wall that separated us from the hall. The boys were permitted to use the restroom just across the hall on their own. We needed to go to the adjoining building to get drinks; and in this case we would all line up and go through the covered walkway to the fountain. It was a relief to have the bathroom nearby. These were the times before the excessive use of bottled water, or we could have had drinks more available. The boys were still on the playground with the regular students. Howard did not seem to engage in play with the others. He was a loner, but there occurred a number of accidents in which Howard was involved. The boys seemed to be in the way when Howard did things. They came back from recess with bumps and bruises attributed to contact from Howard. One boy was struck "accidentally" by Howard's yo-yo when they had both been on the monkey bars. Objects belonging to Howard were often the subject of accidents that produced a lump or bruise from time to time. Each boy believed that Howard was not at fault, that it was totally accidental. The accidents persisted. I saw nothing in Howard's behavior that would indicate that he was at fault.

One day two of the boys had asked to use the restroom. Howard had gone first. When the second boy asked, I assumed that Howard was about to return so I sent the second child. In just a few moments the second boy returned holding his head. The door had slammed on him and a large bump was rising. I looked at Howard. He said he was coming out of the door and did not know the other boy was entering. Both boys said it was an accident. I was suspicious, so I took Howard aside and told him of my concern. I said that too many "accidents" were happening and that he always seemed to be a part of them. I managed to get eye-contact with him and suggested that he held much anger toward the others because he did not feel well accepted. I suggested that the rest room door was used on purpose. I said, "You are very good at getting back at the others without them knowing you are doing it on purpose". Surprisingly, Howard finally showed some emotion. He said he had deliberately hit the other boy with the door and that he was very angry with all of them. They were not friendly to him. We talked about other ways to handle his anger and he started verbalizing his annoyance without inflicting the physical injuries. Howard began to be more social and to improve in his communications.

After the afternoon recess one day, Howard came in with a caterpillar in his hand. The boys all gathered around to look at it. Howard was so pleased that he had something they were all interested in. He said the caterpillar was his friend, some of them laughed. Howard was defiant.

"It is so." he said, "He is my friend and he is trained, he can do tricks"

"Do tricks?" questioned Bobby. "What tricks can a caterpillar do?"

"I'll show you." responded Howard. "Climb up, Little Caterpillar." said Howard.

The caterpillar was on the back of Howard's hand. It started climbing up his arm. This looked rather innocuous to me and I thought it rather clever of Howard. All the boys had gathered around to see Howard's friend. They all watched as the critter climbed up his arm. Howard took him and placed him again at the back of his hand and repeated the direction to the caterpillar.

"Climb up, Little Caterpillar."

He did. This was repeated four or five times. Bobby was the only one who seemed totally unimpressed.

"Of course he climbs UP", said Bobby, disdainfully, "That's what caterpillars do. Tell him to go DOWN."

Howard was perplexed and I was concerned about how Howard could handle this. Apparently he thought he could get the caterpillar to do his will, as he put him up above his elbow and demanded,

"Go down, Little Caterpillar, go down!"

The caterpillar continued his upward climb. Howard repeatedly turned him around and tried to get him to go the opposite direction. I tried to distract the group by starting some directions for the class. Howard became very irritated with the situation and the caterpillar. He smacked the caterpillar hard with his other hand. The caterpillar was dead.

"Oh look!" chided Bobby. "You've killed your best friend".

Howard cried. Of course the boys all laughed. It took some time to handle the situation, caution Bobby, soothe Howard, and give serious counsel to the group.

At the end of the day we had drawing time. Howard made a beautiful picture that I still have. It was carefully drawn and colored with crayon. There was a stage with a table upon it. On top of the table was a little worm-like figure, Howard's caterpillar. At the bottom of the picture was an audience, mostly just heads drawn. It was very good, artistically. There was a balloon above the caterpillar that had the word, "Yeah!" Under the picture was the caption, "The people say 'Yeah' for Howard".

Perhaps Howard has learned to handle some of his frustrations with expressive art, an obvious talent, and that the people somewhere are saying "yeah" for him. He became integrated into regular classrooms the following year, and seemed to be doing well when I left the program.

Three Bird Day

I was so glad that I had received so much information on the learning disabilities of children, as Rene was much involved with all the areas of deficit that we had discussed. Rene joined our class in the spring of the first year. He was one of the youngest in the program and had not made any progress in his first grade class. He should have been in grade two. Rene was quite large at birth and had a very large head. It still appeared large when we got him at age seven. His was a very difficult birth, and he had brain damage at birth that affected his learning skills. He had problems with visual perception and auditory perception, problems with directionality, and memory problems. Most of the children that I worked with in later years seemed to have one specific problem, sometimes two, but Rene had all areas of his learning impaired.

Rene had little academic information. He did not even know the alphabet or numbers. We had a sand table in the classroom, for play and for therapy. I used the sand for kinesthetic enhancement to help him learn letters and numerals. We traced them in the sand. I also made sand letters on cardboard for him to see and feel. He had problems with visual discrimination. I asked him what he saw on the paper where he was reading. He described the letters and numbers and mentioned the "circles". I asked about the circles and showed him a period. Yes, they were a lot like the periods but larger and not as dark. They covered some of the writing. We used a lot of the products from "DLM" (Developmental Learning Materials). These were manipulative pictures and objects made for visual training to assist in improving visual discrimination and memory. Rene began reading. He must have been quite intelligent as he was learning rapidly and had so many deterrents.

Rene's mother mentioned that he had very serious problems with memory, just for everyday things. She said he was embarrassed and would not engage in conversation with guests or even answer the phone at home. I talked with Rene and he said that something really weird had happened. He was talking to his dad, went to get a cookie for both of them. He came back, put the cookie for his dad on the arm of the sofa, and then went to play. When he came back, the cookie was still there, but his dad called on the phone and his dad was in Chicago. Apparently, Rene's problem with memory was as confusing as his visual inabilities. Rene was afraid to answer the phone because he would forget who called, when, and what they wanted.

Rene's problems with memory were related to time, but also to space. One day, the second year he was in the program, he was late to school. His mother called and said that he had started out on his bike and had gone the wrong way. His mother wanted to call to him and stop him, but his father insisted that she not be so protective, and to let him learn. More than an hour later, Rene appeared at school quite tired and confused. He was also very upset about losing his way. He had stopped someone, asked for directions, and got himself turned around. I stayed in touch with Rene's mother for a number of years after he left our program. When he was in high school the family went on vacation to Hawaii. His mother reported that Rene had gone for a walk on the beach and was gone almost all night. When he returned, his feet were scratched and bleeding from the sand. He had lost his direction and had walked many hours, barefoot on the sand, before finding his way back to their motel.

I found out in his second year in the program that there was also a problem with his hearing. We had viewed a film in class, and when my colleague Jan was rewinding she let the film run backwards. The boys were really enjoying the replay and then Rene commented to me, "Hey, the sound is backwards too!" It had been running that way for about five minutes. I said, "That's right, Rene—did you just now notice it?"

When he responded with a yes, I asked him how it had sounded to him. He said it sounded really confusing and messed up, like when I gave him directions sometimes, and he didn't understand them. I made more concerted effort to assure that Rene was understanding from then on.

For Rene's instruction I initially used sand paper letters, the sand table, audio tapes of letter names, tracing of letters, and finally flashcards. Later, he would have audio tapes of words, with the word and the spelling, to accompany his writing practice. He did much work at home with the tapes, worksheets and books. Tapes were used for his math skills also. His mother read aloud with him and read science and social study materials to him. He progressed quite quickly.

Because Rene and I developed a very close relationship with my being involved in how he saw, heard, and remembered. He felt I knew everything going on in his head. One day he came to school and seemed more distracted than usual. He also seemed unhappy. I asked him if he were distressed. He replied that he was, that this was going to be a three bird day, and he said accusingly, "*You* know what that means." I replied that I did not. He insisted that it was in my knowledge. I told him that I did not know some things. I asked him about the birds. He replied that if you see a bird flying, that is fine. If you see two of them in the air, that is alright also. But, if you see three birds together that is very bad and it is going to be an awful day. We talked about how he could change his ideas about what might happen, and focus on good things as we went on in the school day. I did not see a bad three bird day. I don't think that Rene did either.

Rene had all of the areas of reception impaired. He was a rapid learner in spite of his difficulties. It makes one wonder how he would have done had he not had visual, auditory, and memory skills affected by his difficult birth. I used all of the information that I had learned to teach him. I would often ask him how he was able to recognize a word or solve a problem. His insight into what helped him to gather information was invaluable to me in teaching him. From Rene on, I would question my students about how they were able to process information, and then help them to use their strengths to help them gain additional information and skills. As an old wise woman (me) once said, about teaching, "If you wish to fill the vessel, you must first seek the opening."

When Rene first came to the program his complexion had a definite pallor. There was no color in his cheeks. He had a tanned face but the color was flat. He rarely smiled, and often seemed perplexed. He was only animated when we had art. He loved to draw and paint and seemed to have an ability in this. He did many nice pictures in both crayon and paint. At Christmas time, Rene gave me a ceramic gift that he had made. He and his mother attended ceramic classes together and Rene had made a lovely lipstick holder. It had cats painted on it and holes to hold four different tubes of lipstick. I still have that gift. Rene commented one day that he would be a famous artist when he grew up. "Not", he said, "like this," as he showed me a picture of a Picasso painting. He said very positively, "I want to be a *real* artist. I want to do work like the famous paintings of the old masters".

Rene was in the program throughout the elementary grades. He was able to read at grade level by the time he was in grade four, and he was integrated into the regular classroom at that time for some of his academic studies. He was in regular physical education classes and played with the regular classroom students on the playground at lunches and recess. As he became more animated the pallor in his face was replaced by a nice flush from running, or excitement. Rene was in regular classes for middle and high school. I kept in touch with his mother, attended his graduation, and learned later that Rene had gone to Europe to study art. I was impressed to see a painting, a portrait, that he had done. It did look like one of the old masters. He had learned oil painting, with advanced techniques in glazing and use of varnishes, that made it look old and like a reproduction of a great painter's work. He was selling some of his work at that time. I believe that Rene became quite "normal" and I hope that he has had a good life.

Karma?

Ray was one of the younger and smaller boys. He was the same age as my youngest daughter, they had been playmates. I knew Ray before, as Ray's mother was a teacher friend of mine. She taught music at the elementary level. I had enrolled my two daughters in a summer music program that included a children's choir that would sing at an outdoor production of a musical in the park. Ray's mother, Flo, was the choir director. I was involved in the adult choir, as was Flo. We became close friends. Flo was working on her masters degree at a university some fifty miles away. She was attending classes there several times a week. Her busy schedule, both choirs, university classes, and the commute to her school was causing her excessive stress and making her asthma worse. She had to stop at the local hospital to get a treatment for her breathing, on several occasions when she was driving home,

Flo had three boys, one was ten and the twins were seven. Ray was one of the twins. He had hydrocephalus when he was born, and there was a stint in his head that came down through his neck. In certain positions you could see the raised area from the stint. Ray's head was somewhat enlarged and he had trouble learning to walk, run, ride a trike, etc. as his balance was poor. He had a helmet that he wore most of the time, and always for play. I did not know it at the time, but Flo's husband was very abusive and she and her boys were fearful of him.

Flo and I got together and let our children play while we had coffee breaks and conversation that summer. I babysat for Flo a few times when she went to her university for classes. Ray had quite a sense of humor and my girls loved him. Our families got together for barbeques twice that summer.

A mutual friend of mine and Flo's called me one Saturday morning with the startling news that Flo had died. It seems that she had gone to class on Friday, had to stop for help with her breathing, and spent a difficult night with her asthma. She had gotten up early Saturday morning to get her inhaler, which was on the top of the refrigerator in the kitchen. She had collapsed beside the fridge. Her husband found her dead later that morning. I learned from this mutual friend that Flo often had very large bruises on her thighs where her husband had kicked her. He was also very physical with their sons.

After Flo's funeral, her husband called several times and tried to make some time for the children to play together. I was now rather fearful of him and did not want the friendship to continue. I felt very bad about her childrens' loss. I wished there were someway I could continue seeing Ray as I had started helping him with some learning skills. Not that fall, but the next, when I started my new class with the disturbed children, I was shocked to see that Ray was one of my students. My devotion to Flo and my desire to help her son had magically come to fruition, as I was now able to help him.

Ray was like the class clown. He had something funny to say about everything. Ray no longer wore the helmet to protect his head. His head was a bit larger than normal which made his eyes seem larger also. He had a rather wise look with a high forehead and a shock of straight, fine brown hair that stuck up when he had not combed it. He was smaller than his twin and a bit small for grade two. He had been a problem in his first grade class, and the powers that made decisions had staffed him into the disturbed classroom. He had a number of behavioral problems that we needed to work on. He was, naturally, very fragile after losing his mother. He cried often, could not abide any teasing, and so this was not a good placement for that reason. The younger boys were not as prone to disparaging remarks and taunting as my older students were. They seemed to appreciate Ray as he had a good sense of humor and was very sociable. Being in a family with three boys had helped him learn to get along with other boys. His grandmother was doing a lot of the care-taking and she was also quite affectionate with him. He seemed glad that I was his teacher as we had some pleasant history together. He had a "case" on my youngest daughter and often asked about how she was doing in school. They were about the same age.

Ray spent a lot of time trying to be beside me in school. This diminished as he became more comfortable with the classmates. He needed the mother—teacher attention less and less. He was becoming a "boy's boy". Some one had remarked to him at some time about a "split personality". He mentioned this term when there was a discussion about whether someone was brain injured or emotionally disturbed. He said, "Are we split because we are only half here?" He had a rather mature sense of humor. Ray began integration into the regular classroom very early in his stay. His grandmother had spent some time tutoring him, and he was not far below his grade expectancy. He loved reading. I knew that his mother had read a lot to her boys and instilled in them an appreciation for literature. He always loved it when I read to the class and he would snuggle up close to me. I hoped that Flo knew I was trying to watch out for her boy.

Reading was one of the first subjects that Ray wanted to try in the regular classroom. He did well and the class that he entered took a liking to him. He did have a winning personality. He was integrated more and more. His behavior improved, less and less crying and sadness, and fewer and fewer outbursts of anger. Ray was able to move to the regular class by the end of the year.

Over the years, because the educational community was smaller in those days, I was able to find out about Ray's progress. He did well throughout elementary school. I didn't hear about him again until he was grown. There was a news item on the television that had him included in the story. I don't remember what part he played or what the news was featuring. I do remember that Ray was a custodian or caretaker in charge at a company, that the story was about, and that he was interviewed. He looked normal, not such a large head and rather handsome. I did hear that his two brothers went on to college. I think that Ray progressed well in the private sector workplace. I believe Flo would have been proud.

I Am In Charge

Brook was in my second year class of these special boys. He was a very nervous and frightened child. He had a strange pallor that is often seen in severely disturbed folks. He had no color in his cheeks and his face was usually without expression. Brook was a very shy and sensitive boy from a rather unusual family. His father was a musician on a local television show, and seemed rather effeminate. His mother was the more aggressive and outgoing of the two. Brook was an only child and had been indulged in with clothes, toys, and activities. Both parents seemed quite frustrated that he was not doing well in school. He was very bright and they had great expectations for him. He was quite nervous and seemed to have difficulty concentrating. He was phobic about school attendance. He had many fears, it was difficult to know what things were upsetting him. He had lunged out of the classroom a number of times. I was able to catch him most of the time but he did manage to get all the way home on several occasions. His parents were counseled, by the social worker in the program, to bring him back and he finally saw the futility in this behavior, but he did still run from the class when something triggered his anxiety.

One day, something set Brook off and he fled from the classroom. I had taken the boys on several "science" walks on previous days. The walks were out past the playground and on into a field that had a small canal that was almost dry. The canal ran under a bridge where there was vehicle traffic. I was amused and found that it was ironic that the boys, all having severe problems with reading, were able to read all of the obscene graffiti words written on the canal wall. A fellow student in one of my college psychology classes was amused at this phenomenon also. We discussed a possibility of rewriting pre-primers using the words that both of our student populations seemed able to decode. The boys loved the canal with the small wildlife subjects, and the bridge was very impressive. I was unable to catch Brook as he fled, but I did see him head in the direction of the canal. I asked Jim, the teacher next door, to keep an eye on my boys while I hurried to the principal's office. Her office was in the next wing, and back in those days there were no phones in the classroom. It was also long before cell phones were in use.

The principal was a woman. This was unusual back in the sixties in this district. We teachers all used to laugh about the fact that if a man just stayed with the district for a few years he would automatically be moved up to a principal position. Samantha,was the current principal's name. She was in her forties and rather heavy. She also, because of her aggressiveness and short hair cut, seemed rather masculine. She would always say at the beginning of the school year, "You may call me Sam. I will always be Sam. I hope I will not always be Miss Dugan". As far as I know she is probably deceased by now and is still Miss Dugan. I approached her with the information that Brook had escaped once again. I asked her if she could watch my class while I went to find him. I said that I thought I knew where he had gone and it would not take long. She seemed annoyed and said that she was in charge, please tell her where I thought he was and *she* would get him. I told her I was quite sure he had gone to the canal and was probably under the bridge. I went back to my class.

It was shortly before lunchtime. I thanked Jim, finished some work with the students, and got them lined up to go to lunch. The cafeteria was in the main building where the principals office was. That wing also had the gymnasium, the library, nurses station, teachers lounge, and main office. After taking the boys to the cafeteria, I went to the teachers' lounge for my own lunch. Soon there was a lot of commotion in the adjoining room, the nurses station. There was horribly loud screaming and loud scolding from an adult voice. "Oh-oh," I thought, "the retrieval of Brook did not go well." The noises got louder and the yelling more angry with distorted words. I waited for things to subside as I knew the principal would want to handle this herself. I waited and waited. It did not stop. The teachers were all unsettled, and I explained to them that one of my students had run away and that Sam had gone after him. Finally, I could bear it no longer as there was not just the yelling but distinct crying and bawling very, very loud. I went into the room. Brook was absolutely terrified and his face all red, wet, and swollen. I went over to him and put my arm around him and spoke to him softly. He stopped crying and yelling immediately. Sam looked at me with surprise. She left and I stayed and soothed Brook enough that he was able to tell me why he ran, (it was something that Bobby had said.) and he was able to go get his lunch.

Sam asked me what I did to stop his tantrum. I told her that he was just extremely frightened and that I tried to make him feel more secure. She was still angry. It seems that not only did Brook not want to be drug back to school (he *was* under the bridge) but her anger at him escalated the fear and he lashed out against her. Her comment to me was; "No child is going to call me a "Mother F————-". I'm not sure she gained a better understanding of severe anxiety attacks or terror in children.

Red

The second year that I had Brook, he still did not want to be at school. He had to be watched or he would dart out of the classroom and head for home. He had gotten better after his running away several times the first year, and when he had the confrontation with the principal, but the new students, new classroom in a different wing of the building, brought back much of his anxiety.

This was the year that we were in the hall closet with the ripply glass walls. It was necessary for me to place myself between the door and Brook so that I could deter any lunges from the class room. Brook would relax after a period of time. He would get interested in the class procedures or his own work and stop the pursuit toward the door. The education experts had determined that it was beneficial to use carrels (three sided plywood structures with a built in shelf for a desk) with troubled children. I had one for each of the boys in my already crowded and small room. I bought some play phones and we played "office" for the school day. The boys had pride in their office and seemed more interested in doing their school work. I pretended to be their secretary when handing out their assignments. The individual tutoring sessions were like a conference and I would occasionally tell them of a pretend phone call that they needed to take. Group work was hard with the structures but the good outweighed the bad. Once or twice a week, Jan and I would organize an art class that I would teach to both classes. We used her room as she had a full sized classroom with a sink and large counters.

In our art sessions it became obvious that Brook would not use a red crayon or red paint. In conferencing with his mother, she revealed that Brook would not wear any red clothing. He had hidden a pair of red socks under his dresser and, when she discovered them and asked him about them, he would only say that he hated red. His mother said she thought that it was from an experience he had in watching television. There had been a special on the science channel that told about childbirth. Brook had been allowed to watch, as his mother was trying to be a good mom and give him experience and knowledge. He had become hysterical about the blood shown and she did not know why he had reacted that way. She thought that this had caused his phobia of red.

Brook was so very anxious that he appeared to have anxiety over many things. He was distressed about his school attendance, but had learned to cope with being there. He did manage to escape and run home a couple of times, but seemed to be improving in his tolerance for being in school. We had already had several fire drills. Brook always seemed more nervous when getting in line and moving in or out of the building, and I was quite sure that the extra excitement from the drill was even more upsetting to him. I would always have him next to me and held his hand whenever I could. When the monthly drill with the actual firetruck arrived another problem was discovered. Brook turned very pale, wide eyed, and ran. I caught up with him in the adjoining building. He was terrified. He acknowledged that he was afraid of the fire engine. In speaking again to his mother, we both decided that he was fearful of it because it was red.

The next time the fire drill was done with the fire department, I had prior knowledge and managed to have my class in an area away from the street where Brook would not see the engine. This worked well, but the next time the principal did not know of the drill, as it was the surprise one that the fire department did on occasion. Brook had gotten so much better about staying in school that I had let him leave the classroom for a drink—on his own! He did not return and I went from the classroom to find him. He was lying face down on the cement walk on the way to the main building. The red fire engine was parked within his view, on the street about twenty yards away. The fire bell had not yet rung. Brook's little hands were gripping at the cement and were scratched and bleeding where he had dug them into the walk. He was stiff and totally terrified. I helped him up and took him back to our room. In consoling and calming him we talked about his fear. He revealed that it was not because it was red, it was because it was a fire engine, and red reminded him of fire engines. It seems he had told his mother that he hated school so much that he wished it would burn down. She told him how awful that was that he wished the school to burn, and about how awful it would be for all the poor children to be burned alive. He had such guilt that when he saw the fire engine he thought about the possibility of a fire. All the children would be burned and killed—and it was because he wished it. After considerable reasoning and counseling with Brook, He was able to tolerate a fire drill.

I had Brook again the next year. When the class was moved the fourth year into the church building, Brook was no longer in the program. I don't know if he were integrated back into a regular classroom or if the parents had found alternative education for him. I did run into him and his family after he was no longer in my class. There was a community gathering at one of the city parks for a firework celebration. Brook was there sitting with his mom and dad on a blanket. He smiled and spoke. His family was friendly. I did ask where he was attending school. His mother named one of the buildings in the district. It was inappropriate for me to ask about his progress with him sitting there. Brook did still seem rather anxious, still pale and with low affect. I'm not sure how well he adjusted. I do know that the family had gone into a family counseling situation. I still wonder how things turned out for Brook.

I'm Sorry

Mike was a tough kid. He was in my first group the first year. I am surprised that Bobby was able to intimidate him as, even though Mike was smaller, he was strong and did not like anyone bossing him. Mike had a black, nylon jacket that he wore most of the time. Even when it was warm outside, Mike had his jacket on. It was his security. I was able to talk it off of him in his more comfortable moments, but I mostly let Mike alone with his jacket when he appeared to need it. Mike did not converse much with the other boys. He did not confide much with me.

His parents were also thrifty with information or communication. Mike did as he was asked, most of the time. There were several occasions when I had to take him by the arm and place him in his chair, when he had gotten aggressive with the other boys. His reason for admittance into the program was primarily academic failure and lack of motivation. There was some defiant behavior and aggression also. Mike was mostly quiet and behaved better than some of the others in the class. I did not know what was troubling him other than his lack of academic skills.

It was spring, close to Mothers Day. I had some time to give the boys an art period. I asked them if they would like to make a card for their mothers. Not such a great idea! We talked about Sunday and what Mothers' Day was all about. Some of the boys seemed eager to make a card. It was their art period and I had gotten some special construction paper and stickers for them to use. I instructed them to make a card, if they wished, or they could make a picture or use our clay.

Mike sat immersed in his coat with his head down. The others went to the counter to paint, get paper or clay. All of them except Mike opted to make a card. They were all talking about their work and I watched Mike become more and more irritated. He readjusted his coat a number of times and mostly kept his head down. After a period of time I approached Mike and asked him if he would like to do some other artwork and gave him some suggestions. He was now not just irritated but out and out angry, at all of us. Mike got up from his desk, coat still on, and thundered over to the counter to get some colored paper. "I'll make your dumb card" he said in a very angry and loud tone. He went to his desk. Everyone left Mike alone as we all did when a classmate needed to unwind or de-escalate. Mike worked quietly and angrily by himself. Near the end of the period, Mike, still hunched in his coat, approached me and handed me the card he had been making. He later said he did not want to give it to his mother, that I could just "keep it". That is what I did. I showed it to the group's social worker to help in Mike's family's counseling, and I developed a better understanding of Mike and his needs.

The card was a construction paper folded to make a card. The front had a drawing of a boy with horns on his head and a very mean look on his face. It read simply, "I'm Sorry". Inside were some other hastily done drawings of a boy, books, pencils, school, etc. The inside had more disturbing messages. It read, "I'm dumb. I'm sorry I wuz ever borne. I will lev if you want."

Mike was the oldest child in his family, he was tested at a minimally retarded range that explained his academic difficulties. He felt he was a disappointment to his parents. We had a lot to work on aside from his academics.

Picasso

Phil was one of the original students in my first class. He was short for his age, had small bones and appeared to be a child with "failure-to-thrive syndrome". He was nine and turned eleven during his stay in the special class. Phillip was so small he would be assumed to be only five or six years old. He also acted quite young. He wanted to be near the teacher most of the time and even tried to sit on my lap. When I took the class to assemblies or any other meetings with larger groups, Phillip would sidle up to me, lean on me and often try to climb up in my lap. I assumed that his mother was probably still holding him on *her* lap. His mother expressed not just concern for Phillip's behavior but also fear. She told me that Phillip had tried to kill her and her husband. When I expressed lack of belief, she continued with details to substantiate her concerns. It seem that while his father was sleeping on the couch and mother was upstairs, Phillip had turned on the gas in the kitchen stove. The burners were not turned on nor the oven lit. The gas was pouring out into the house. His mother discovered the leaking as she smelled it on arriving in the kitchen. Phillip had no response to the questioning of why he had done this. He did not deny that it was he who had turned it on. I commented to his mom that perhaps he did not understand the danger or know about natural gas. Her response was that he certainly did. He had been instructed about the stove, gas, *and* the dangers. "So," she continued, "He meant to kill us. That was his intention". Phil was hard to understand. He seemed friendly, even affectionate. He was anxious and moved about rather quickly, often upsetting, spilling things, or knocking them off surfaces. Once, when I was getting into my desk drawer, Phillip appeared suddenly and slammed the desk drawer closed. I barely got my hand out in time. I had turned to Phil, saying angrily, "If you had caught my hand in that drawer, you would have had to pick yourself up off the floor!" When this story was related to our social worker, he was concerned and said that I really did not mean that. I responded that, yes, I did. If I had been suddenly hurt intentionally, as Phillip was trying to do, I'm sure I would have lashed out, if the pain would have allowed it. It was a very hard strong slam of the drawer. Phil seemed to be a little concerned about me after that. He was careful and more obedient and respectful. I wondered if he possibly had intentionally turned the gas on at his home. As he was the smallest child in the room, he did not react aggressively toward the other children. In fact, when Bobby was on his bully kick, Bobby was Phillip's protector. Bobby threatened the others about any possible mistreatment of his small buddy. I watched to see if Phillip had set up this relationship. If he had it must have happened out on the playground where I was not privy to the conversations.

The boys took turns handing out the morning snack of milk and a graham cracker. One day in the week when it was Phillip's turn to be snack helper, he had left the room to go to the restroom in the hallway. The boys were permitted to go alone to the restroom as it had not been a problem. This day Phillip did not return in a timely manner. More time passed and I became concerned. Bobby suggested that maybe Phil was constipated. I stifled a smile. I asked Bobby to go down the hall and check on Phil to see why he was taking so long. Bobby came back with a huge smile and then a cringe on his face. "The little jerk got in the toilet and he was playing with his turd—in his hands! He was using it like clay—making a sculpture or something" Bobby had told him to flush it and wash his hands. He came in a few minutes later, and I repeated the instructions to wash his hands, adding that he should be very thorough. I quieted the boys and talked with Phillip about bathroom cleanliness. The class was tittering about Phil's actions, and the incident took some counseling for both the class and Phillip. The boys were now waiting for their snack. Phillip started to do his assignment and a cry went out from his classmates, "don't let him touch my food". I told Phillip that under the circumstances I thought we should have another monitor—just for today. He was completely embarrassed, so he easily accepted this. For a while after this incident, Phillip had to be accompanied by an older classmate, of his choosing, when he went to use the restroom.

Phillip was quite an actor, on several occasions he acted like a dog. He would bark, growl, and snarl at his classmates. They were sometimes amused, never alarmed, and often just ignored him. I went along with the charade and gave him his classwork and called him over to his desk with, "Come here, boy. Climb up here and do your math". He would bark and yip in a friendly way, run to his desk (on all fours) and then climb up into his chair. He would then do his work as directed. We all knew that Phil liked playing a dog and I assumed it was "play".

Phil came to school one morning and was completely silent. He did not speak to anyone. He seemed very upset and I asked him if he would like to talk. When I got a positive response, I asked my teacher neighbor, Jim, to watch my boys for a few minutes while I took Phil outside on the stoop for a little counseling. Phillip finally started to cry and shared that he felt that he was so bad that nobody liked him. I told him this was not so. His answer was that I did not know what a terrible thing he had done the previous night. I told him that I would like to hear about it, that I was sure it was not all that terrible. It took him a while to relate the story. It seems that Phil's younger brother and he had spied upon some relatives that were staying at Phil's house. Phillip's mother was so horrified when she caught the two of them that she berated the boys all evening, and had put most of the blame on Phillip who was the family bad guy, and also a year older than the brother. Then Phillip said it was not just that they spied, it was that they had seen things that his mother said boys should not see. They were "nasty, dirty, horrible boys" that had caused her deep embarrassment. It seems that the two relatives, man and wife, were staying in a guest room that had a transom window above the door. The boys were doing what boys do, trying to peek to see what couples do in their bedroom. The woman was having her menstrual period and was changing her pad on the bed. Phillip had a hard time trying to explain the very terrible thing that he had seen that should never have been observed by such horrible, nasty boys. He was terrified in explaining what he saw. I tried to assuage Phil's guilt by letting him know that this was a normal thing that he had seen, not dirty, or nasty, and that he was not nasty and dirty, but that he *was* guilty of peeking at people who were trying to be private. He and his brother should not have climbed up to look in their window, but what they saw was not their problem. He was only guilty of violating the privacy of the guests. The woman should have been in the bathroom but the boys *were* wrong in having peeked. Phillip was upset over this incident for several days.

Besides being a dog, Phillip liked to be Superman. He asked me to call him Clark Kent and he called me Lois Lane. I would give him some worksheets and he would say, "Thanks, Lois." We carried this on for a number of days. One day, when it was my turn on playground duty, Phil came running up to me with a friend he had found from grade three. "He is not really Superman, is he?" questioned the young boy. Phil was pleading with me to confirm his identity. I explained to the boy that Phillip liked to pretend he was Superman, and that he called me Lois Lane. It was a game of pretend that we were having. Phillip looked a little dismayed but seemed to accept my response to his newly found friend. I assumed that Phillip knew it was pretend and understood that the boys in the class were indulging in our pretense.

Phillip could be so very theatrical. When we were having an art lesson, he dramatically splashed the paint on his paper that was on an easel. He did it so precisely and intentionally that we were all kidding him about being a *real* artist. For the next week, I brought some of my oil paints, a panel, and brushes I also brought a large shirt for him to cover his clothes to avoid stains. He dramatically splashed the paint on the panel. He made a very impressionist painting of a forest with lots of varying shades of greens and yellows. It appeared to have a path taking you into a deep woods. I stopped him from painting when the work appeared "finished", in order to stop him from destroying the great image that he had created. We put Phillip's painting in the next school art show and he won a prize. At this time, Phillip began telling us all that he *was* Picasso. I finally realized that he was completely involved in the identities of dog, Superman, and Picasso. To him it was more than a game.

In discussing Phillip with the social worker, that oversaw our program, I learned he had counseled with the parents, and knew the story of the attempted gas poisoning. He was concerned about the level of reality that Phillip possessed. He said, "If you said, 'will the real Phillip Stein please stand up', you might be horrified at what would be there".

The third year of the program, Phillip was in Jan's room. He came up to me on the playground in an almost hysterical frame of mind. He had several students following him and calling to him. He ran off. They asked me if I knew what Phil had in his hand. I did not. They were upset and said that he was crazy. I called to Phil, and when came back, I asked him what he was holding. He flashed a small matchbox at me and said, "See what this is?" I asked him to show me. He flashed it again this time flicking the box quickly opening and shutting it. There was a small wad of hair inside. I asked, "What is this, Phil?"

"It is my mother's hair" he responded in an eery voice. Jan and I reported the incident to the social worker. He also was quite concerned.

Phillip's family moved away the next year and we never heard the result of his therapy or his next placement. I ran into Phillip the following year in a large department store. He was now twelve and still appeared to be six or seven. He was holding on to his father's hand like a much younger child. Phillip was probably one of the most disturbed children that I had in the program. I do not know of his outcome.

Expletives

Marshal was a tall, attractive boy from grade three. He had been suspended from regular classrooms because of his constant swearing. He was given numerous punishments to no avail. His parents were extremely frustrated. They felt that everyone thought that their home was one of continual bad language. Marshal did not respond to any of their disciplinary attempts. He was almost at his grade level for his academic skills. His problem was that his attendance in regular programs was out of the question. He swore at any startling occasion. If he dropped his pencil, made an error on his paper, stumbled over something (often done on purpose so that he could come out with an outburst), or any surprising or negative occasion, out would come the swear words. He was very bright, interesting to talk with, and pleasant, except for his swearing. We had many discussions on why this was not acceptable behavior for school. Marshal was one of the new students in my third year of the program. We were housed in the hall electronic equipment closet, the one with the ripply glass walls. This is where Brook had made numerous escapes. Marshal used these Brook-escape occasions to come out with his well planned swear words.

As the boys were scholastically able to handle integration into a regular classroom, they were given the opportunity to join in another class for the subject at which they were proficient. Marshal could handle any of the third grade academics. I let him choose the subject for which he could integrate into a regular class. He picked science and we had a long discussion with him and with the regular classroom teacher about his language. She let him know that, if there were any obscene outbursts, he would leave the class immediately and not be permitted to return. Marshal accepted the plan and he and I practiced by keeping a schedule of the amount of time that expired between his swearings. When his control seemed appropriate for a class period, he was allowed to join the other class. He came back quite proud of himself and the other boys cheered. We had a number of talks about how nice it would be to belong to a regular class and not be in a special program. He seemed to be quite interested in changing his behavior, and getting back to his home school. He was concerned that his past classmates would remember his poor behavior and ridicule him. We talked about gradually entering more class periods here in *our* school and not to worry about his old classroom.

Marshal was lengthening his periods between swearing outbursts. He would get involved in his own schoolwork and sometimes forget that he was supposed to swear at sudden noises or movements. He enjoyed going to science and we extended his visits to the math class. He was doing very well. The third grade class where he attended seemed to be accepting him and wanting him to come in their group more often. He was, as I said, bright and interesting. He was tall with dark wavy hair and beautiful bright blue eyes. It seems that several of his girl classmates in the new group had gotten a crush on Marshal. His loyalties and interests were gradually moving from our group to the regular classroom. Our boys were very proud of Marshal, and I am sure they thought about how it would be to start integration themselves.

One day, Marshal was quite engrossed in his seat work and Brook knocked over the teacher's chair next to my desk. The loud bang made everyone jump and look up. I think we were all waiting for Marshal's usual, "Well, God Damnit, What the Hell was that?" or one of his similar outbursts. He looked up, startled, and said very loudly, "Well, Mercy A-Mighty". We were all pleasantly astonished. Marshal had never said anything like that. Then we all laughed loudly. "Well, Marshal", I said in admiration," I believe you are just about ready to be *in* a regular class." He smiled appreciatively.

Marshal moved into more and more classes with the third grade. He made no mistakes. He was fully integrated by the end of the school year. The next year reports from his home school were very favorable. There had been some family problems that had provoked Marshal's swearing problem in the beginning and the family counseling was continuing. Marshal had found acceptance.

Chapter Six

WORKING WITH THE LEARNING DISABLED

After I had completed a year at the university working on my doctorate, I returned to my school district and was assigned a position teaching reading under a federal program. As a corrective reading teacher I was now blessed with the knowledge from learning disabilities training, of determining what was impeding a student's ability to grasp the written language. I used the information about visual perceptual problems, auditory problems, and memory deficits to help me ascertain with what problems the students were coping. I believe that this made me a more effective reading teacher. I had three grade level classes (comprised of grades three, four and five) and they were large. It seems to me that the more the schools implement new approaches to reading, the more many students are unable to gain from the class instruction. Every twenty or so years it appears that those making decisions on how to teach reading decide to throw out the use of phonics. While phonics usage does not help all students, it does seem necessary for some. Those students with memory problems who cannot see a word and recall it later, and those who have some visual perception problems and do not consistently see the same image or it is distorted, need something to assist them in decoding the word *each* time it appears. I believe strongly in phonics instruction and have seen it help many students who were previously non-readers.

After the corrective reading assignment year was over I returned to the university with a leave of absence from my school district and another research assistant-ship from my university. I again worked on my doctorate, worked with grant programs, oversaw student teachers, and taught university classes. I truly enjoyed my work there and was offered a position at the end of the academic year. I thought seriously about moving to a university level. It was a long hard decision. I would have to take a cut in pay as beginning college instructors do not earn much, especially if they have not published and do not have a "name in their field". Most of all I had really missed teaching children. I made the decision to return to my school district.

There was now a huge influx of teachers into the new field of "learning disabilities". My district had hired a number of these new teachers, some of them had been my students at the university. Each L.D. teacher had at least two elementary schools to serve. I had two and was assigned to give assessments in a third school. We L.D. teachers were to teach Monday through Thursday and to spend Fridays at the huge district staffing sessions, if we were involved in any staffings, or to spend the time testing and writing up test results, for students referred for the program at our individual schools. We also had an afternoon meeting of the L.D. teachers biweekly to keep us informed and work out any problems with the new programs. None of us had very many students as the program was just beginning, and assessments had to be made before the placements. As our enrollments grew we were gradually moved to servicing only one school.

Later, with national focus on what caused the problems, and the acceptance that the child must have either birth defects or not have progressed in correct sequence in his beginning sensory skill, the classification of the program was changed to "Perceptual, Communicative Disorders" or PCD. We were admonished to not teach academics but to train the child for balance, eye hand coordination, hearing discrimination, or visual perceptual skills. Beginning reading, language, and math workbooks were put away and PCD teachers were advised to use special DLM materials (a large producer of "Developmental Learning Materials"). We all had balance beams, wiffle balls, workbooks of visual designs, memory cards, etc. There were a number of us who felt that the academics needed to be included, and we quietly continued to work on reading and math skills. This movement lasted for a couple of years and then we returned to academic focus. I maintained some of the perceptual training skills in my program to a small degree. When I retired many years later, there were two teachers for learning problems in almost all of the elementary schools. However, they were later to become special education teachers for the "moderate needs" programs. The "needs" were whatever problem the child exhibited, mild retardation, perceptual problems, memory problems, behavioral problems (affecting learning), autism, or whatever.

The biggest problem in servicing the Learning Disabilities was a space to work. We teachers used whatever we could find or wherever the principal decided he/she could allow. Initially some of the instruction was to be done with the child in the regular classroom. This was also a "national Idea" with very little positive result. I was only able to achieve a good result with one placement. The classroom teacher was a good friend and she taught at the front of the room, I at the back. We both kept our instruction on a quiet level so as not to interfere with each other. My time in her classroom was during the reading instruction period so that we were both teaching reading. I had only three of her children staffed into my program. We agreed that I would also instruct four more of her struggling students. We had a very positive outcome for the joint effort.

LD teachers were using hallways, closets, basements, or any area that they could find. I did instruct in several different school basements, by the furnace room, I also had a shower room in a school where there used to be showers for the P.E. programs. It was back by the kitchen storage room. I had several closets that were in hallways the most memorable being the "vomit closet". It was named by my students as it was the custodian's closet for storage of toilet tissue, mops, pails, chemicals, and so forth. It also had a large floor sink where the custodian could wash out his mops after cleaning up areas. Because of the sink for vomit clean up, the kids titled it the vomit closet. This closet also had a ladder that went to the roof with a trap door above. This was partly to enable the custodian to climb to the roof to retrieve any balls that got misplaced up there, and partly to check on the venting system. There was a small slit around the trap door through which one could see daylight. We had a small table made of a plank with metal legs attached. It was adult level. We also had three folding adult sized chairs, so I was able to service two students at a time if needed. The table was shaky, as were the chairs. There was only one dirty shelf, that the custodian did not use, where I could put any books, workbooks, paper and such.

One winter morning when I arrived for work, it was snowing quite hard. The snow was coming in through the sides of the trap door and a puddle of water lay on the floor. I had battled my own allergies and those of my students with the dust from the dust mops and other paraphernalia. But now you could actually see the snowflakes coming down from the cracks in the ceiling around the trap door. School had started and I wondered how we could get much done with the flakes and the puddle on the floor. I was highly discouraged. School had started and I decided I needed to go pick up my first two students. I stopped on the way to complain to my friend, a first grade teacher, in the classroom right next to me. She had begun instruction with her students, but I decided to interrupt her. "Oh," I complained, "You should see my 'room' now. It has snow coming in and there is a big puddle on the floor". I was puzzled as she smiled and nodded and looked very uncomfortable. I glanced to the side of the room, and there sat the principal. My friend was being "observed". I was a little embarrassed for the teacher, not for myself, as I was now angry. I walked over to the principal and spoke somewhat softly telling her about the snow and water. She only gave me an angry look and said, "Move out into the hallway for the day".

My coworkers were annoyed about my place of instruction and one of them made a sign and put it on the door over the "custodian" sign. It said DR. LANCER. The principal never seemed to notice. One day the assistant superintendent came to visit our school. It was on a day when I was out testing another student at a different school. This man was the most concerned administrator that I had ever encountered. One of the teachers in the vomit room hallway showed him where I worked, even opened the door to show my furniture and the room contents. That afternoon I went to the large staffing session at the administration board room. There was my principal. She was one of the "permanent members" of the large district staffing team I described earlier. My principal came over to where I was sitting just before she left. She leaned down and whispered, "I want you to move into the media center today. Dr. C. did not like where you were teaching". She had a big smile as if it were her doing that I should be moved. The media center space was much better. It was off the media center itself, a small alcove with a sink for hand washing, as it was the entry way to the boys and girls bathrooms. I did receive an instruction table and three chairs, child sized. This was great!

I had the good luck of having small rooms, usually used for speech therapists or conferences, from time to time. Then after teaching for many years, a classroom was divided during the summer construction, in the off school months. It would be used for my program and the school counselor. I got to choose. Did I want the half that had the outside door and the chalkboard, or did I want the side that had the sink and cupboards? I chose the sink side and a chalkboard was put on the wall between the classrooms. I had a sink. I loved it. I could let the kids have free time with art projects! I used the sink also to make hot chocolate in the winter and we had occasional tea parties the rest of the year. Several times I had students say we could just move in and live there, since we had heat, electricity, water, sink, comfortable bean bag chairs (that I purchased), and the bathrooms were right across the hall. We all felt very "at home". I got to keep this room for my instruction until retirement, some fifteen years later. I did have to share it with a speech therapist and a psychologist later on. But this made a wonderful, comfortable place to help my kids be able to learn.

Chapter Seven

MY LD KIDS

Looking Normal

𝒫amela was a clever, bright second grader when first I met her. This was early in the tenure of the "learning disabilities" programs in our district. We were assigned a case load but had no office or small conference space in which to do our instruction. Some of the district principals had decided that we specialists should work in the classroom with the teacher and other students. This was a poor decision for a working situation with little Pam. She had a very rigid and determined teacher. The personality of this teacher can be seen by the following story;

There was a surprise fire drill with the fire department. The school was graded each month on such a procedure. The time was monitored and reported in the fire department records—and I suspect to the school administration. It happened to be on a very cold and snowy day back in the time when children really bundled up for bad weather. This teacher was very concerned for her students and made them all put on their snow boots, coats, gloves, scarves, hats, etc. This took some time. Meanwhile the other classrooms were exiting the building. Other teachers led their groups out in single file and all were waiting outside, in the bitter cold, with no coats, for the bell to ring to signal a reentering of the classes. They had to wait an especially long time in the cold, as this concerned teacher was not outside for the "count". It took some time to help dress the second graders and get them lined up. The school record for clearing the building would have a poor showing. When confronted with the expected and correct procedure, the teacher firmly announced, "I am not going to jeopardize my students health for a fire drill".

So this is the teacher that was to have Pam receiving individual instruction at the back of her classroom. Pam totally understood the teacher's personality and reveled in being as disruptive with this procedure as she could. The teacher consistently called out *my* name along with Pam's requesting consideration and quiet. Pam smiled and was obviously pleased with her attempts to upset the teacher, embarrass me, and get revenge for having to be singled out as having 'learning problems".

Luckily, the next semester I was assigned a small classroom that was no longer in use by the school counselor. Pam would walk down two hallways to come to my room for her scheduled time.

Pam's mother had taken her to an eye-doctor who diagnosed a condition of "myleopia", Also called "lazy eye". Her eyes were not working cooperatively together. The remedy used during this period of time was to cover the weaker eye with a patch to rest it. Pam was very distressed about having to wear the flesh-colored patch over her eye. She said she didn't want to look "not normal". I had a great solution for her. After checking with her mother, we decided that I could draw an eye on the top of the patch. I was a part time artist, an art major in college, and at times a portrait painter. The eye that I drew was very correct and real looking. I used colored pencils and made it look very much like Pam's other eye. She was impressed, her classmates were impressed, and now somewhat jealous. As for her teacher, I wouldn't want to bet on any positive reaction.

With a quiet, non-invasive classroom, Pam was very attentive and learned quickly. I only had her for two years. During that time we colored a lot of eye patches. She would come to my room before school and get her new daily patch ready. After moving on, Pam stayed in touch for a number of years—into her adulthood. On a gift giving occasion, Pam gave me a small glass elephant. It was carefully wrapped in one of her eye-patch boxes. I was so touched I kept both the box and the statue.

About twenty years later, Pam had married, had two boys, and returned to live in the school neighborhood in her mothers house. Her father had terminal cancer and she and her husband and kids had come to stay with her mother. She came to school to visit me and wanted to know if the school was a good placement for her oldest son. Her boy would be entering kindergarten and was already reading. I assured her that we had a very exemplary kindergarten teacher who seemed able to teach each child on his/her own level. This teacher managed a lot of individual instruction. Pam requested this particular teacher and put Elam in her class.

We talked for a time and I told her that I still had the glass elephant that she had given me but had long since discarded the cardboard eye-patch box. She laughed and said that she had kept one of the eye-patches, on which I had drawn her eye, with her personal keepsakes.

Elam was very bright and he qualified for the Gifted and Talented program. When he got to the third grade he was in my special program for creative writing that I taught for the gifted program. He wrote a number of beautiful and very thoughtful poems. Pam printed one that was published in a nationwide children's anthology and put it in a lovely frame for his grandmother. Pam had another boy while they were living in our district. I went to her home to see the new baby. All three of her boys were very bright and beautiful and Pam was a very loving and creative mother. The family moved back to the state where they had been living, as Pam's husband found a good job there. I hated to see them move and have not heard from Pam for a while. I still have the glass elephant.

I Fell

My working space was for a while in the old library. This was a room half the size of regular classroom. It had been built for a library back in the days when there were few books for a library and there was no instruction given there. I shared the room with a speech therapist and we tried to coordinate use of space and group instruction time. Jesse was one of my younger students. He was a first grader who was so physically attractive that everyone noticed him. He had light blonde hair with one great wave that naturally went back from his face. He was physically well built, and well coordinated. He had the appearance of a child model. His parents were very proud of Jesse and very concerned that he was exhibiting less than perfect skills in learning. They dressed him impeccably. He was like a miniature cowboy hero. He wore expensive jeans, cowboy boots and western tailored shirts. He looked "well dressed" but not comfortable.

Jesse was a little shy. He tried very hard. He wanted to please his very involved parents. He seemed a little stressed from the expectations put upon him. He was an only child and in meeting with the parents, they let everyone know that Jesse was the apple of their eyes. Jessie tried so hard and he was starting to make progress, gaining word recognition of new words from day to day.

One morning when Jesse arrived, there was a very large bruise on the side of his face. It was alarming in its size and color. I of course asked Jesse what had happened. "Oh," he said, "I fell down". It was hard to realize how the boy could have fallen on his face, and how it could have caused such a bruise. I asked if he had hurt any other part of him. He showed me his leg with another large bruise. I questioned him again about the fall. Had he fallen against a sharp or hard object? He seemed confused and just repeated that he had fallen down. Any suspicious injuries were always to be reported to the nurse for observation. I dismissed Jesse's classmates and walked with him down to the nurses station. She asked him the same questions as I had. He again just repeated that he had a fall. We went back to class and I talked with him again. I let him know that the nurse was just concerned about his safety and questioned him again about what had hit his face. He started to whine a little and then choked off a sob. "My dad," he said through the tears starting to come down his bruised cheek, "He hit me with a board. We were fixing the car and he got mad. He didn't mean to hit me. I think the board just slipped out and it hit me. He said to tell the school that I fell" After dismissing Jesse, I returned to the office and talked to the nurse. I also stopped in and briefly explained the situation to the principal, who was noticeably upset.

The office referred the situation to child protective services. I learned at my lunchtime that help was coming for Jesse. The principal had left for his morning conference at the administration building and was no longer available. This was a good thing, as Jesse's father was visited by the authorities who had come to investigate possible child abuse. His father was so angry that he went immediately to school and demanded to see the principal. The principal was not in his office and the father thundered past the secretary to see the empty office, and then rushed into the nurses station. He issued all kind of physical threats. He was descriptive in what he wanted to do to the principal who was stupid enough to think that he would hurt his beloved child. The police were called. The end of the matter was that it was determined from interviews with parents, Jesse, and school personnel, that charges would be filed against the father. He finally admitted that, in a fit of anger, he had struck his son with a nearby two by four. The car he was working on had fallen off the blocks and hurt the dad. He took his anger out on Jesse, as his son was with him, and the dad thought that Jesse had pushed something. Jesse was taken from school. The authorities were involved and I assume that, at least, parenting classes were mandated. Jesse returned some weeks later, without his bruises. No one gave us any information about how the case was finally resolved. Jesse never mentioned the situation again. He continued to work hard, dress beautifully and I hope continue to be the apple of his (more self-controlled) parents' eyes.

Choose Me

All the teachers in the lower hallway (grades one through three) knew Lisa. She was a holy terror. Even all the paraprofessionals who manned the cafeteria and the playground had endured confrontations with Lisa, or had at least heard about her. She was not intimidated by anyone, not even the principal. She was extremely outspoken and given to bursts of anger and throwing things, usually books or crayons. It was near the end of the school year and we had a staffing for Lisa. Everyone of the teachers in grades four and five could only feel lucky that they did not yet have to deal with her. She was extremely bright and appeared more than self confident for a child that qualified for special help in academic achievement. She was in first grade and not learning to read very easily. It was a puzzle to the teachers as she was so clever and quick witted. With testing, it was revealed that she had a moderate amount of dyslexia. This cause of frustration made Lisa even more defiant in her dealing with adults. She had been difficult with many of the paras. One lady remarked to Lisa that her shoes should be buckled. Lisa had on Mary Jane shoes and the straps were hanging loosely. The para was concerned that she would trip over the straps and fall. Lisa's response was that her mother was in charge of her shoes, and she sauntered on down the hall leaving the para somewhat surprised. Another time a para commented on the shortness of Lisa's dress. It was one she had for a while and was obviously outgrown. It was a Tyrolean dress with the laced up bodice and different colored velvet skirt. Lisa told her, "It's a native costume and is supposed to be this way—my mother is in charge of my clothes, you need to deal with her." It came to the point that the paras were somewhat uncomfortable in trying to discipline or advise Lisa.

Smart remarks, angry outbursts, and throwing things were not too serious to me, as I had seen worse in my experience with *very* disturbed children. In one of my earlier exchanges with Lisa, as we began work and we were just getting acquainted, Lisa informed me that she started the day with a cup of coffee and hit off the bong. Her mother and father were separated and Lisa spent much time with a grandmother who adored her. Lisa's mother was much of a "hippie" even though this was in the seventies and the culture much dissolved. Lisa talked about her favorite rock star who was much a product of that generation. Her adult interest in rock music, references to drugs, and indignant behavior made her seem more like a teenager than a young child. Lisa had beautiful dark curly hair and large violet eyes with very long lashes. In her appearance, she was the perfect, pretty little girl that every mother would want her child to be. That difference in her looks and actions was what seemed to upset all the staff. She was a legend in the school at grade one.

Lisa was having a very bad day. She had words with her regular classroom teacher and had been extra defiant. He teacher had sent her down to my classroom so that I could counsel with her. Of course she was not too happy to be there, as it was the end of the day, and Lisa told me that she had an art class that she was to attend right after school. We talked for a while and Lisa became defiant about having to come see me although we had been getting along just fine. She told me how angry she was at her teacher, at the paras, and the school situation in general. She demanded that I let her leave even though the dismissal bell had not rung. I gave her some directions about what we had to settle before she left. She had gotten out some magic markers and was drawing on a large paper. She promptly drew on the desk top and then threw the markers to the floor.

"O.K., Lisa", I said firmly. "You may leave as soon as you wash the marks off the desk and pick up the markers and put them away."

"You just want me to be late don't you? You are making me miss my class. I am not going to do that. I am going to leave."

"No, you are not". I responded firmly, placing myself between her and the door. I repeated what she needed to do before leaving—and then the bell rang.

Lisa continued a tirade, accusing me of wanting to stop her from attending her art class. I made no other remarks other than repeating what she needed to do and that she had time to get to her class if she conformed to my demands.

"You know what you are?" she almost yelled. "This is what you are. Look! This is what you are!"

I did not look up and continued to ignore her. I was now seated between her and the door and was doing some paper work. I continued to not look at her. She had to tell me what she wanted me to see.

"See, this is you. You are the middle finger!"

I still said nothing and just waited her out. Soon she got up. She went to the sink and got soap and a sponge and came back and washed off the desk. She put away the markers. Then she took the sponge and began washing off all the desks and the counters in the room.

"Lisa", I said quietly, "That is fine. You did what I asked you to do. You need to leave now. You don't want to be late."

"That's O.K." she remarked calmly. "I just wanted to help you. I can do this. I won't be too late."

Lisa continued cleaning the classroom for a while and then left hurriedly. We were even better friends after this standoff. I assumed that Lisa probably had her mother and grandmother under her control with her temper tantrums, and she appreciated some discipline.

One day Lisa appeared at my door with a carrot in her hand. She smiled slyly and put the carrot to her mouth.

"MM mm—What's up, Doc?" she asked, mimicking Bugs Bunny.

Lisa had asked me about being "Doctor Lancer" and I explained my title to her. She asked if she could call me "Doc". I told her that was fine. It gradually changed to Docky and was adopted by the other students. Later the custodians, cooks, some of the teachers, and even the current principal called me Docky.

Lisa worked hard and her grades came up to above average before she was staffed out of my program. In the meantime, Lisa became one of my most cooperative students. She had her birthday only a few days from mine, and when we discovered this Lisa asked if we could celebrate together with a cup of tea and some cookies. We both brought goodies and sat together and had a small birthday celebration. The next year she asked if we could do this again. I was happy to do so. She requested that I wear a dress for the occasion (most teachers were wearing pants at this time). I did wear a dress and we had a wonderful tea party. On several occasions Lisa had asked me if I thought she were "bad". Of course I told her she was not, that she did some things that upset the adults around her, but she was not a bad person. In fact, I told her I had seen a lot of understanding toward other children coming from her. I thought she was basically very sweet and considerate. She smiled and then thoughtfully looked off into space. Speaking quietly, she said,

"Docky, if you die before I do, would you help God choose me for Heaven?"

I stayed in touch with Lisa for a number of years. When she was in high school she had a lot of problems. She did get involved in drugs. The last time that I heard from Lisa she was back at home with her grandmother but she had been in a half-way house. She said she had been to "the very depths" but had risen and was so glad that she had overcome the demons that had plagued her. I heard that she had been heavily into drugs, had born a baby, and been in rehab. The Lisa that I knew was an extremely bright and caring girl who could be very loving. I remember her as very charming, beautiful, clever, and very, very special. I would surely help in her "choosing". However, as the great poet, Lancer (me) once wrote:

> What does God use, when he does choose
> The souls for Heaven bent?
> For only some can overcome
> The trials they were sent.

Bouncing

Neva was a beautiful, graceful young girl of eight years. She had a face with delicate features and beautiful blue eyes and blonde hair. Her hair was wispy and soft and she wore it long and strait. She was slender and rather small for her age. She had a very innocent look and would have made an excellent model for an angel or fairy. She had just moved into the school district and had been living in the eastern edge of the state where there had been a rash of reported incidents of satanic involvement. Neva had a severe problem with sexual disturbance. Her mother did not report her masturbation activities until the school brought it to her attention, then she said that Neva had exhibited this problem in her prior school, and that the family was seeking help at the local children's hospital. I was seeing Neva as she had been diagnosed at her prior school as having learning disabilities. I had an hour daily scheduled with her.

Both her third grade teacher and I were given permission for exchange of information with Neva's therapist at the hospital.

Neva's third grade teacher was a very understanding person and had much tolerance for children with problems. The teacher placed her at the back of the classroom where the children would not be so aware of her activities. Neva would rub herself and move her body about. She called it her "bouncing" and she was very upset that she could not control herself. She talked with me and her teacher and cried when she said, "If I do this three times in the morning I will not bounce". She demonstrated putting her hands together, as in prayer, and then raising her arms up over head, down through her body and then back up over her head, three times. Her teacher and I had an agreement that Neva could come and be in my room at any time, if she found it difficult to control the "bouncing". Needless to say I spent much time with Neva.

Conversations with her psychotherapist at the city hospital for children, revealed that this had been a problem for at least the last year. Parents were aware and trying to get her help. We wondered why they had not made the school aware of her sexual problem and just mentioned the learning disabilities. Her therapist at this point was unaware of the cause and was working with both parents. Over some time the therapist found out from Neva that she had been sexually assaulted by a girlfriend's father. This person was a neighbor and it seemed very strange, that with this revelation, the father was not so angered that he would go out where they had lived—only about thirty miles away—and confront the man.

Parent teacher conferences revealed a very unemotional and apparently disinterested father. He sat on the side of his chair and turned his back when I talked to him. His responses were single words if at all. Neva's mother was more involved but very nervous and uncomfortable. She seemed very concerned and wanted to know what she could do, other than the counseling they were receiving at the hospital. I let her know that we were working closely with the child psychiatrist at the hospital and that we were making accommodations at school for the problem. Parents were told that Neva could come to my room when she felt out of control. Her classroom teacher was at the conference, and later her classroom teacher and I discussed the remoteness of the father and nervousness of the mother.

As the year progressed, the psychiatrist suggested giving Neva some clay to have in her desk and suggested that she manipulate the clay when the urge to bounce came upon her. This was not very effective. Use of the clay had not been a distraction, and Neva had responded better to leaving the class and going to another location. Neva did become able to stay in her classroom for more and more time, as she became more comfortable in her new school.

Neva would talk a lot to me about her problem and seemed angry at me from time to time after she had revealed information. Once she became hysterical after making a visit to the girls' rest room across the hall. She was crying and out of control and said that there was a bloody, dead baby on the floor in one of the stalls. I told her I would go and check. What she had interpreted as a baby was a super market plastic bag in a hump. It had some red print on it that she had wrongly perceived as blood. When I explained the situation to her she became calm, but it took a while. In reporting this incidence, (and the fact that she also drew a dead baby and a dead rabbit on a piece of paper) to her therapist, we decided that a meeting was needed to discuss the possibility of satanic cult involvement.

Her therapist joined our school nurse, the classroom teacher, our principal, and myself in a trip to a police administrative building to talk with an officer who was in charge of the satanic cult movement in our area. He gave us much information and he felt that Neva's bouncing, the plastic bag incident, and her drawings were very suspect. He also recounted the number of satanic incidences in the suburban area from which Neva had moved. We were all suspicious that the molestation by the girlfriend's father was not the complete picture. Neva's therapist and I discussed the possibility that some sexual abuse was still happening. She had complained to me that her "private area" hurt. The school nurse was reticent to examine her because of possible lawsuits. We were pondering all adult members in her home, mother, father, and the live-in grandmother. They all verbally presented themselves as very concerned and unable to give any helpful information about Neva's problem.

One day, Neva came to school particularly upset and asked her teacher if she could come to see me. She related a very upsetting dream that was still with her into mid-morning. She dreamed she was having her birthday party (this was coming up in the near future) and she was trying to shower and get ready for her guests. In her dream the shower was filled with feces and the water was filthy coming from the spigot. She tried to clean it out but more and more feces kept coming into the shower stall, and she was covered with the mess. She kept crying, "I couldn't clean up the poop". What a classical dream! After much consoling, she was able to go back to her class. Each time we had sharing moments like this Neva would become rather distant and sometimes angry toward me.

Once Neva drew a picture on the chalkboard of a girl and then put vertical lines all across it. She angrily said, "This is not ME! I know you think it is me, but it is not. It isn't anybody. It is just a drawing." The officer that gave us the information on the cults had said the victims were often caged and were afraid of bars. He also said that in their rituals they would use costumes of cartoon characters, like Mickey Mouse and Donald Duck, so when the victims were trying to report these incidents to anyone it would seem unreal, like they had had nightmares or were delusional. He also revealed that persecutors were often dressed as police officers, so that the victims would be frightened of the police and would not seek police help. At one point when Neva was telling me how hard it was to stop the bouncing, she said, "I know you think that someone is touching me or hurting me, but they are not. No one is bothering me. I'm just a bad person and so I bounce." I had never even intimidated to her that I did think this. Her concept of being a "bad person" was consistent with earlier remarks about her inability to control her bouncing. Her report of the way she needed to raise her arms in prayer ask for help was also filled with remarks stating that if she could be a good person it would all go away.

For some unknown reason, a police officer came to school to talk with Neva. He was in uniform. Neva was terrified. The school office had called Neva to the conference room and when she became hysterical the principal, who was not informed of this, brought her to me to calm her down. After the explosive incident and calming Neva, I went to the office. The officer was still there. He had been told Neva's family might be in a cult. He was given a piece of my mind while the principal stood silently by. The principal was unaware of the visit as the office personnel had sent for the child at the officer's request. We never found out why he had come or who had sent him. This incident was very traumatic for Neva and she remained upset throughout the day. I called her mother after school and got permission to drive her home. When we were only about three blocks from her house a police car passed us. Neva became hysterical and dived under the dashboard for concealment. This, too, seemed to be confirmation of a cult involvement by her family.

The psychiatrist and the school continued to cooperate and Neva seemed to respond. She spent less and less time in my room and more time with her regular class. She seemed to get the bouncing pretty well under control. Her academics came up and she was performing at grade level. Neva and her family moved the next year and although I stayed in touch with her by phone, I didn't see her again until she graduated from high school. Parents and Neva had reported her progress to me, by phone and by Christmas cards, and told how very well Neva was doing.

I was invited to Neva's graduation. I sent a card but did not attend. During that summer I was invited to a shower for Neva. She was getting married. I did go to her house for the party. I met her fiance and a number of her friends. She was a lovely, beautiful young lady with all the correct social graces and seemed to be quite well adjusted. Her family was gracious and more communicative than in the past. Everything appeared fine.

I never saw or heard from Neva again. From my knowledge and experience, I would expect that some problems arose in her adjustments to marriage, child bearing, or even becoming a well adjusted adult. I hope that good things continued to happen for Neva.

To Feel Better

There was a very dedicated black female, grade-five teacher. She had a new student, a black boy who had been tested and needed to be seen in my program. The teacher was concerned because the boy, Darin, was so quiet. She said his father had been on the nearby large city's police force. His mother was a teacher in that city's school district. They had recently moved to our suburb. Darin's teacher said that he was having trouble concentrating. He did little or no academic work, and yet she had no problems with him as far as behaviors went. He was not very social with the other fifth graders and seemed depressed. I put him in my fifth grade group.

Darin was with four other fifth grade boys. Two of them were also black and I assumed that the small group would help Darin to make friends, adjust to school, and participate more in his regular class. It did not seem to help. Darin stayed much to himself. He was shy and mostly very inward in his reaction to his surroundings. He did not smile often and needed to be encouraged to share any ideas or knowledge in his group. It came time for the parent conferences and Darin's teacher asked if I would meet jointly with her and Darin's mother. His father did not sign up for conferencing. We scheduled the time and I was interested in getting some ideas from his mother to help Darin.

The classroom teacher often included her fifth grade students in her parent conferences. Darin was invited to attend. We all sat uncomfortably in the student chairs near Darin's desk. We introduced ourselves, the teacher mentioned strong points in Darin's behavior. She said how positive he had become in approaching his learning tasks, how dedicated he now was in turning in assignments, and then said she was concerned that he did not seem happy at school. We all discussed how difficult it is to make a school change, particularly at Darin's grade level. We talked about ways to make new friendships and asked how we could work with him in finding other boys with whom he could be a friend. I noticed that Darin kept scratching at his leg. The scratching continued and seemed to get more violent as the topic proceeded to the discussion of his academic shortcomings. Then, as Darin moved his hand back up to the table level, I noticed blood on his fingers. I interrupted the conversation and asked Darin if there were a sore on his leg. His mother demanded to look at it. There, on his leg, was a rather large hole that

Darin had dug, and dug at while we were talking. He was intentionally hurting himself.

Darin always wore long sleeves and it was later revealed that Darin had numerous sores and scars that he had produced by digging his nails into his arms and legs. I told his mother that this was a serious concern and that Darin was in need of some intense counseling. She and her husband both took the opportunity to find someone to deal with the entire family. She realized from what Darin had said at our conference, that he felt he was a severe disappointment to his parents. They told us that his older brother was succeeding at everything, and that Darin felt that he was a failure at everything. His mother had been in tears as she realized the pain that her son was feeling. I was surprised that, with the numerous sores and scars on both his arms and legs, that neither parent had noticed them. Darin's age and his seclusive behaviors, along with the busy schedules of the parents had caused the problem to be unrecognized. In times I spent discussing his problems with Darin he told me how very bad he had been feeling. He said he was feeling better now that his parents were concerned for him. He said the pressure for school achievement had been alleviated. He said, "Sometimes when you hurt so bad on the inside, it helps a little to make a sudden bad hurt on your outside. I guess I just did that to myself to feel better."

Sometimes in wanting our children to succeed, we don't realize the pressure it can cause them in knowing they feel inadequate in meeting our expectations and we cause them great internal grief. I have seen a lot of frustration and inner sorrow from my students regarding their inabilities. Much sadness is from their own dissatisfaction with their performance, but even more often it is from them feeling that they have let down their parents.

A Future Great Poet

Shannon entered my program in the third grade. She was almost a non-reader. She was new to our school district and had been diagnosed at her former school. She was very sweet, very sociable, and worked hard but her visual perceptual problems were severe. When Shannon wrote, her letters were often placed one on top of another. Words were inconsistent in their appearance to her eyes and her mind. I stressed phonics with Shannon. Her doctors had said that she was not in need of glasses, but I thought that the earlier approaches in handling visual perceptual problems might have been helpful to her. I had one student that the eye doctor had said, his eyes were seeing things each one differently. A special prescription had greatly improved his reading abilities. That seemed to be the case with Shannon as she could not get her hand to put the letters next to one another, rather than on top of each other. I felt that she might not be seeing correctly, but she had been examined and the doctors said her eyesight was fine. There must have been confusion in the transferring of the information to the brain.

Shannon was extremely bright and had great insight into others and their actions. She was a joy to have in class. All of her classmates loved her.

I worked hard with Shannon. She learned phonics and became very adept at "sounding out words". This helped as her visual constancy and visual memory were problems. She would see a word and not recognize it as one that she had seen before. In addition to phonics skills, she worked with flash cards to help her develop a base of sight words on which to rely. Shannon was in my class for grades three through five. At the end of the fifth grade Shannon was reading at about grade three level. She sounded words frequently and so her reading was labored.

My sister who was dyslexic as a child would send me information on dyslexia that she would find from time to time. Her son was severely dyslexic and had been unable to read until grade eleven. He suddenly was able to read and he became a fluent and avid reader. No one ever knew what had changed for him. He had to have his books read to him until this time. One of the informative studies that my sister sent to me, linked dyslexia to food allergies. I was suspicious about Shannon's diet, and also any psychological problems that could be affecting her abilities. Her parents worked opposite shifts. He mother worked nights and Shannon related that she was fearful when her mother was gone. She wore a large jacket that belonged to her father. She said that she would cling to her dad when mom was not there at night. She reminded me of Mike that I had in the emotionally handicapped classroom. His anxieties had kept him all bundled up in his jacket for protection. Shannon had her fathers huge jacket to protect her. She was a beautiful child with very long ash blonde hair that she sometimes braided to make the ridges in her almost wild looking tresses. She had large, wide, innocent eyes and always a ready smile. I did a lovely portrait of Shannon that I still plan to give to her one day.

One winter morning, Shannon came to class and when we started our oral reading, she was reading fluently with no need to stop and sound out a word. I was surprised, as was she. I had just been reading the study about diet being a source of dyslexia. I asked Shannon what she had had for breakfast. She reported that she had not eaten anything so far, on this day. She had awakened late and hurriedly got ready and left for school. She just had not had time. Since Shannon was now in fifth grade and rather independent in her thinking, I felt that she was old enough to give her information about a possible diet connection to her disability. I hoped that she would confer with her mother and they would investigate the possibility. Nothing happened. Shannon continued to read slowly and sound many words. After a week or so Shannon came to class and again read easily. "Wow," I said, "what happened Shannon? You are really reading well today." She laughed and said, "I didn't eat anything again." I approached her mother about this and suggested a food allergy problem. Her mother did not follow up. Shannon, I believe was coping with other problems that took precedent in her mind.

Until she was in fifth grade, I did not know that Shannon was experiencing problems at home. Her mother was overly protective and did not even let her walk alone to school. She only lived three short blocks away and the neighborhood was quite safe. One of Shannon's classmates gave me this information that Shannon had never disclosed. The friend was concerned about how Shannon could adjust to going to middle school. She felt Shannon would be ridiculed if everyone knew that she had to have her mother escort her to class. I spoke to Shannon about this and she said her mother was adamant in her position and would not let her go alone. I did not know if this problem were Shannon's or her mother's. The friend also told me that she was suspicious that Shannon's mother was abusing her. I saw no bruises or marks and gave Shannon lots of opportunities to tell me if she had a problem in this regard. Nothing was ever disclosed.

Although Shannon had much difficulty in putting her ideas in writing, she had a great talent for expressing herself in words. She wrote beautiful poetry and sometimes I could not decipher her writing and would need to have her read it to me. We entered one of her lovely poems into a contest for children's poetry. She had her poem accepted and it was published in the poetry anthology. The poem was written when she was in fifth grade, yet it sounded more like an adult's work. I was with her as she was developing it, so that I knew it was her own. After that fine poem, she wrote a number of others that were very good. Some of them revealing her fear and loneliness.

When Shannon went to middle school she had a very good L.D. teacher who was especially interested in her case. This teacher continued to encourage Shannon's creativity and she helped Shannon to submit another poem that was accepted for publishing. She now had two poems published in national anthologies. This was a great source of pride for a young lady who still experienced much difficulty in just reading. Her reading level did not increase much and Shannon began using the resources for the blind and had access to books on tape. She moved to another state, and because her grandparents lived near our school, she came and visited them in the summers. When she was in town Shannon would call me and she would come and visit me.

Shannon continued to use books on tape throughout her high school years. She also continued to write. She had work published again several times. When she came to visit me after her graduation from high school, I learned that she had "lettered" in forensics. I had always thought that forensics referred to crime solving. It seems that she went to regional contests for her writing. She read her poems aloud and was given a "letter" for accomplishment in writing. I asked if she was now reading. She said that she could, although it was hard. She still was using taped books. She could read for things that were necessary. She was now an adult and felt that she could trust me with the information that I had always suspected. Her mother was abusive, both physically and emotionally. Shannon was hit often. She never had bruises that showed. Her mother and father were finally separated and Shannon was living with her father. She still had much anger toward her mother. I have not seen Shannon for a few years. I heard that one of her grandparents had died and that Shannon was living in their house. She was married and had a baby. This information was given to me from one of my students in my volunteering program. My student asked me if I knew Shannon and said that she lived near Shannon, and that Shannon had said to say hello to me. I will try to contact her as I have some of her poems that I promised to give to her. I am hoping that she still does creative writing.

Only If I'm Paid

For several years each, on several occasions, the schools where I was working made use of what they called "care teams". These teams were composed of a group of volunteer teachers and staff that were engaged in helping solve problems with the difficult students in the school. The volunteers were often prompted to volunteer because of their positions. So, usually the team included the school psychologist, the school counselor, and any other specialists in the field. The principals would sometimes come to team meetings, especially if the child being discussed was of great importance to the school climate. I served on these teams when they were in existence. The principals would try to get members from each of the grade levels to join. This way we had a number of different views on the behavioral problems. The teams usually met weekly and addressed referrals from the staff. The classroom teacher who was responsible for the student referred was also in attendance. We discussed ways of helping the child with his problems, and gave suggestions to the classroom teacher. These meetings were usually the first indication that a child needed a referral for testing, and possible placement into a special service.

Such was the case with Jacob. He was an angelic appearing third grader with less than angelic behavior. Several teachers came to our meeting to discuss Jacob. He was seen as a very badly behaving child with great anger inside. He had thrown a chair at the classroom teacher, had anger outbursts in the "specials", (art, music, and P.E. classes), and had also been a problem on the playground and cafeteria. Even the cook was concerned.

Jacob was not large for his age. He had rather small bones and a beautiful face. He had large blue eyes with extremely long lashes and a cherubic mouth. His blonde hair was softly curled and fell over his wide forehead. He surely looked innocent. It was determined that Jacob should be tested and interviewed by the psychologist to see what his problem could be. I did academic testing although the teacher had said he was very bright and read well, he produced little in the way of written work. His writing was very "sloppy" and he often refused to perform. He threw crayons and pencils and yelled out at fellow students during written work time. It was not surprising, his visual perceptual skills were very poor. Jacob was good at art but penmanship was much like that of Shannon's. He had letters of varying sizes, not evenly spaced or straight on the lines of the paper. He mixed capitals with lower case letters and often overlapped the letters. It would seem like disregard or sloppiness to parents and teachers who were not aware of eye-hand coordination/visual perceptual problems, mostly because he was good in art class. The psychologist found a lot of anger, as suspected. Jacob did not like school. He felt the teachers were stupid and also the classmates, the principal, and everyone involved. Initially I believe that the psychologist and I were also in this category.

Jacob, himself, was not stupid and he knew it. He was extremely frustrated. He was frustrated with himself and others because they could not help him. He tested above the one hundred fifty I.Q. level that was the ceiling on the psychologist's test. My academic testing showed his math, reading, language, social studies and science levels to be at the high school level. The one defining test indicated that Jacob's spelling ability was at grade three, his current placement. Because of his very high intelligence and other high academics, Jacob qualified for "learning disabilities" with his comparative low score in spelling and his poor handwriting skills. So, Jacob was my new student. His mother and father both came to the staffing session and were both relieved that we had found the source of Jacob's great frustration. In talking with Jacob, I believe that he knew all the time and did not want others to realize his inabilities in writing and spelling. There was also a visual memory problem that inhibited Jacob from remembering word forms to reproduce them. His reading level was so high, as was his understanding of written information, that it was hard to believe he could not produce the language. He just could not spell, or put the work on paper. We spent most of his class time with phonics instruction. Because of his intellectual ability, Jacob could learn the rules of phonics when he could not visualize the word to write. He was quite resistant. He acted as though all this nonsense were beneath him. He did mellow out as he saw the improvement in his ability to express himself on paper.

The psychologist who tested Jacob worked with me to get him identified as a "gifted and talented" student. We needed questionnaires from teachers, parent, and Jacob, along with the I.Q. test scores. The questionnaires addressed the talented area. Jacob did know he was talented. His mother surely did. His teacher was still quite negative about Jacob as she was the one who had received the desk that hit her leg. The art teacher gave him a good recommendation. We were able to put him in the more positive special gifted program along with the L.D. placement.

Jacob was sure of his other abilities. One Friday when the class had free time, Jacob elected to play with some clay that I kept for art time. He turned to one of his classmates and inquired, "would you like for me to immortalize you in clay?" I smiled at Jacob and said, "You are too late, I have already done that in oils". I paint portraits and had pained this girl the year before. Jacob appreciated the humor. He had a very mature use of sarcasm and irony at his young age and was quite entertaining every day. The teachers who had problems with him earlier seemed somewhat fearful of his sharp tongue and defiant attitude.

As he learned to spell and I continued complimenting his new skills, he seemed unimpressed. He did start writing more and started expressing himself with poetry. The writing content was extremely good and very thoughtful. I shared some of it with his mother. She sent a pamphlet to school that Jacob's father had put together with a number of Jacob's earlier poems. He had dictated them to his mother who had been his scribe. His father was an artist and had great computer skills. He had made backgrounds for the individual poems on his computer. I gave his mother some of his new poetry and his father was going to enlarge his booklet. Jacob wrote unusual things. One day when he had finished his assignments and there were just five minutes remaining, I asked him if he could produce a poem in the last few minutes. His written response was a poem that started with, "My teacher said to write a poem, I only have five minutes". The poem was clever and well done. He continued to write lovely poetry and began to slow in his acquisition of phonics skills. He seemed to feel that if he could make an approximation, he could use the spell check on the computer to finalize what he wanted to say. I did ask him to write a poem on a special occasion and got a sarcastic reply. He said that he was sure that he could write something notable, but that he was tired of writing. He said, "I'm not going to write any more poetry until I get paid."

His family moved at the end of the school year. He began attending fourth grade in a nearby school district. It was over a year before I heard about him. I ran into his mother at a bus stop. She said that Jacob was not writing poetry anymore. I was upset as he had such great potential. With the things that went on in his head, I would surmise that he will again be expressing himself with his great language ability. Later that year, a teacher from Jacob's new school district called. She wanted information about Jacob. She did know that he had been in special education classes for learning disabilities. She was surprised that we had also placed him in a gifted child program. She knew he was bright but did not know how extremely bright he was! He was being difficult and she was asking how to "reach him". I told her about his poetry and asked that she consult with the parents about his writing. I did not hear about Jacob again but what a joy he was in enhancing my school experience.

The Children's Hour

I had many doubts about telling this story as this was not my usual experience with students. My career was filled with many pleasant, happy relationships with kids. I am remembering the best. This was a very negative experience that I had and I suppose, although it should maybe not be included in with such fine ones, that it might be beneficial for a reader contemplating teaching, or a beginning teacher to realize that these things do happen. I am sure I had other not so pleasant or successful experiences that I have forgotten over the years. But, I have never forgotten this one.

There were two fifth grade girls that were assigned to my program in my early years of teaching the learning disabled. Both had recently been staffed into the special program and really did not want or appreciate the fact that they would be getting some help. They were in the same fifth grade classroom and neither girl was well accepted socially. The one, more aggressive, girl was even disliked by most of her classmates. She had a competitive personality as far as social skills went. She cared little about academics and much about gossip and back-biting that can be a part of adolescence. She was beginning to act more like a middle school student. She was very concerned about boys, clothing, social relationships, and had even started using makeup. The other girl also had few social skills and was a follower. They had joined forces in gossiping about other girls, fighting over boys, and causing disruptions in their regular classroom.

Because of a rather large caseload, I needed them to be scheduled at the same time as they were older than most of my other students. They were both over a year behind in their reading and language skills, but my other students were in earlier grades and even lower in reading skills. Their classroom teacher did not like the idea of them both going to my program together, as their friendship was already becoming a problem to her and the class. Separate schedules for them would have been more desirable, but I saw no way of placing them separately. I planned to work with them a while and then possibly place the quieter, more compliant girl with one or two younger students, and let her help to tutor the younger ones while still working on her own skills. I had found this to be a very positive experience for other children. In the meantime I was putting up with flippant remarks, late arrivals to class, continual interruptions in class, and little effort.

Their sessions would start with them coming late as they were playing on the way down the long hall, along with the fact that the classroom teacher had to remind them to get started several times. They would enter, giggling and making silly and catty remarks about their classmates. I would try to get them started on their assignments, but they would interrupt the discussion with unnecessary questions and excessive comments. When they did start work, they would stop shortly and ask for help that was obviously not needed, or make comments to one another. I talked at length about classroom behavior and focusing on learning. I resorted to sending "checks" for behavior back to the classroom for the lingering in the halls and late arrival. Things were not getting better. I had discussed with the principal, who approved my scheduling assignments, the fact that I would try to place them with some younger students. She agreed that this was a valid approach. I was still sorting out my rescheduling and decided to try one last effort with the girls. When I had talked with them about behaviors they had denied that they were silly, not getting down to business, and interrupting me and each other needlessly. My plan was to tape the beginning of their class without their knowledge. Then use the remainder of the class to let them hear and then discuss what they were doing. I hoped that they would then decide that, as I had been telling them, they were wasting, their time and mine, and could be learning some better academic skills.

When they entered late at the next session, I had started the tape. Their comments about why they were late, and their giggles were expected. They continued talking, not following instructions given several times, and making unrelated remarks before finally taking their seats, and getting out their materials. I started instruction and was very surprised by the comments that then followed.

"We are mad at you. You caused us to have to go to detention for getting so many checks from you."

"Yeah! you think we play in the hallway. The teacher just forgets to send us. It is not our fault and you give US checks."

As I started to explain my use of checks and the fact that the principal had found them loitering in the hallway on several occasions, Maggie, the more aggressive one, smiled a sly smile, interrupted me and said,

"Yeah! we know what you think. You don't like us. The kids in our class don't like us and we don't care. They should have to go to a special class for reading help. Then we could laugh at them."

Oh dear, I thought, this is a problem with their self esteem being attacked because they are in a special program. I need to deal with this and include their classroom teacher and some instruction for their classmates, the poor girls.

Then Jenny, the more passive and quieter one said,

"You just wait. We are going to get even with you. We have a plan and you are going to get fired."

Maggie tried to quiet her friend but she continued and Maggie joined in to feel as important. The girls expressed that they were going to get me in "big trouble". They had told their mothers about me. They said I would be surprised at what they said, but that their moms believed them and they were going to see me fired.

I had not stopped the tape and so their plan for getting rid of me, and possibly their involvement in "special help" was all recorded. I decided not to confront them with the tape at this time. I quietly asked them to return to their work. After such a revelation and such anger they were quieted and showed more dedication toward their projects than ever before.

The next morning, while still contemplating how to solve the problem, I ran into the principal in the hallway. She stopped long enough to tell me that she had gotten a call from Maggie's mother and that the mother had requested a meeting with me and the principal. She asked when I could come and talk with her about the scheduling. I was not surprised because of what the girls had said. When I went to the principal's office I took the tape recorder. The principal was horrified. She had never heard of such rebellion in an elementary school. We discussed how to proceed. We determined that we should meet with both mothers, listen to their concerns, and then call in the girls and play the tape for all.

I expected to be accused of not liking the girls, as they had remarked, probably giving them checks they did not deserve, and not helping them, as so little was being accomplished. The principal and I sat in complete surprise as the mothers both told how their girls were upset about our class sessions. They said that both girls complained that I asked them lots of personal questions. They said that my class was not helpful, as I spent all my time asking them things about "sex". That I asked them lots of personal things about what they knew, what they did, what the girls in their class did, and so on. The mothers were understandably concerned. Then the principal played the first part of the tape. The mothers acknowledged that there was a lack of focus and misbehavior on the part of their daughters. Then they heard the later part of the tape where the girls bragged about their "plan". The mothers were horrified and very apologetic.

Maggie and Jenny were sent for. They were smiling and seemed delighted until they noticed the expression on their mothers' faces and the stern greetings they received. The tape was played, both girls were alarmed and were squirming on their chairs. They looked at each other and Jenny began to cry. She said it was all Maggie's idea. The principal asked them about the accusations. Jenny said that we had never talked about sex, ever. Maggie was still defiant, until her mother angrily told her that she had embarrassed her own mother by making such allegations and that she would be severely punished. Maggie then also began to cry. She said she was sorry. Her mother demanded that she verbally apologize to me and the principal and that she also needed to write a note asking for forgiveness for such an angry deed. Both mothers left, embarrassed and angry with their girls.

Many years earlier I had seen a movie titled "The Children's Hour" in which some teenage girls in a boarding school had brought some horrible accusations against one of their teachers in an effort to get her dismissed. I wondered if Maggie had seen the movie. It seemed unlikely as it was an old one and a classic. Still Maggie did not seem capable of such a clever and devious plot.

Jenny's family moved before she finished grade five. I still needed to work with Maggie. She was more subdued and cooperative but still did not benefit much from the help afforded her. A few years later Maggie's younger brother was assigned to my classroom. He, too, was behind academically. His social skills were also lacking. He was more amenable to instruction, but was never a good student. He was also not well accepted by his peers and was one of those kids you hear about that was always bullied.

He was in trouble with the law in middle and high school. I do not know how Maggie turned out.

Lost Baby

A new girl entered in the fourth grade class across the hall. She was a pretty child, but very unkempt in her appearance. Her clothes were old and worn, her hair was often messy, and she never appeared clean. The girls in her class were rude to her and made comments about her clothing. She had already been diagnosed as having learning disabilities, so I scheduled her into my program. I put her in with three other fourth graders. The other students seemed to have problems with her. It seems that August, the new girl, was always making comments about their clothes and their appearance. This was probably due to her own concerns of how she was perceived. I heard her taunting two girls from her class, she was saying that they purchased their clothes from the Goodwill Store.

I made a home visit to August's apartment. Her mother was also very defiant and unfriendly. I stood and talked with her outside of her door until she became a little more friendly and invited me in. She had perceived that I really had come only to get help for August. We talked about how she was having difficulty getting along with others, and about her lack of motivation. August's mother was concerned and brought August in from the back bedroom to talk with us. We both tried to tell August that things she said offended the other students, and so they were attacking her in return. I found out that August's mother shopped for her family at the used clothing stores. We tried to impress on August that clothes were not that important. Several weeks later, August had a new pair of shoes. They were one of the prominent and acceptable brands. Her mother must have really stretched her dollars to be able to buy them for August. She was very proud and let everyone know what the brand name was. She also belittled the shoes on the feet of her classmates. We had numerous counseling sessions along with the academics to help August learn how to make friends and be more accepting of herself. Her anger and slashing comments diminished over time, and she began to make some friends. She began tending more to her personal appearance and took pride in trying out different hairstyles, as she was black and had been having just a few messy braids. Soon it seemed that her mother must be helping her, as she had some neat cornrowing styles.

August became less negative about her school work as well as about the other students.

One day, August came to class with a beautiful drawing of a little girl. It was a portrait of her. It seems that August had a father that was an artist. She had become more comfortable with the other students and was able to share with the class that her dad had sent her this drawing. Everyone admired the picture, remarked how pretty August was, and what a good artist her dad was. The next day August brought the letter from her father that had come with the drawing. She read it to us. She also told everyone that she did not live with her father. He sent her letters because he was in jail. The group was very accepting.

I had told my principal about my home visit to August's apartment. She was concerned and asked me to please not go to that building again, without another adult accompanying me. She said, "If you give me some notice, I will go with you." It seems there were several older apartment buildings that housed some rather suspicious characters. One day in her office, she told me that there were about four single mothers living in August's apartment building, who, when she tried to contact them by phone, had the same male voice that answered and took a message for them. The principal was called back, but she said it was quite unusual that they all had the same person to answer and that they were all "unemployed" single moms. She said she suspected that August's mom and the other ladies were working for the man. She said she would not speculate in what capacity. I was even more concerned for August with this knowledge. August had two siblings whose fathers were different from each other, and different from August's. As the year went on, August improved socially and academically. She came back the next year and had problems in grade five in socialization skills. She gained enough academically that she was able to be removed from my program before she entered middle school. It seemed that whenever her placement or circumstances were changed, she resorted to hostile behaviors toward others. I had concerns for her adjustment to middle school. I knew a counselor where she would be attending and asked her to please keep tabs on August.

At our school we would occasionally hear about the former students from staff in the middle and high schools, as the students progressed and graduated we often knew. We heard about August from time to time. I assume she completed high school but am not sure.

A number of years later, there was a news item on television about a young single mother of three. The woman had jaywalked across the busiest street in the city. She and her three little children were struck by a hit-and-run driver. The youngest child was killed. The mother's name was August. She also had the same last name as our August. A picture was shown of her telling about the accident. I was sure that it was the same person from the approximate age and her appearance. Her three children were all from different fathers (reminiscent of her mother?) and although she seemed very distraught over her loss, August still exhibited the deep anger that I had always seen in her. She commented how awful it was for the driver to get away, and how she had lost "her baby". I wondered how she was supporting her children and if she had ever been married. Fellow teachers also remarked that they had seen August in the news and how sad they were for her.

Sandy's Courage

Eduardo, grade five, Sandy, grade four, and a younger than school age sibling, and their parents, all took the flight from a small South American country to the U.S. Eduardo described his first air plane flight. He was very frightened but also pleasantly excited. He told how great he felt it was to be able to come to this country where the doctors could help his sister. He was in my learning disabilities classroom, as he was considerably below grade level in reading and spelling. His math grades were quite good. The English acquisition because of his Hispanic background was surely a main factor. Eduardo was very bright and only needed this one year to pull his reading, language, and spelling up to grade level before moving on to middle school.

Sandy had multiple problems. She was born with spina bifida and her legs were greatly affected. She wore shoes with ankle braces attached to give her legs strength to walk. Her stride was staggered and halting. She leaned far forward in her walk and had very poor balance. She seemed about ready to fall at any time. She did fall on multiple occasions and this was very frightening to her. Sandy's teacher was right across the hall from my classroom. Her teacher was a very understanding and compassionate lady with three children of her own. She was very helpful to Sandy over the year. Sandy was allowed to come into the classroom as soon as she arrived at school on the bus. She was frightened of the busy classroom and had a great fear of falling. We had a staffing for both her and her brother before they started attending. Eduardo was diagnosed with learning disabilities as was Sandy, at their staffing. It was also determined that Sandy's physical disabilities enabled her to have some physical therapy assistance during the school time.

Sandy began her attendance by being on the school grounds before the bell rang in the morning. One morning, she was outside huddling against the building. With the excitement and excess movement of the children around her, she staggered and fell. She became hysterical and one of the paras brought her into the nurse's clinic. I was called to the office to assist. Luckily the nurse was in our school on that day, rather than just a paraprofessional nurse's aide. We both tried to calm

Sandy to no avail. She was crying hard and then her breathing became exaggerated. The nurse tried to call her home. She had determined that Sandy was in danger of going into shock, and was contemplating the need to call emergency. Several phone calls to home resulted in no answer. Because of the financial problems involved, I asked the nurse to call one more time, as the mother had told us at the staffing meeting that she would be available during school hours. I went to find Eduardo on the playground. He responded anxiously and hurried to her side. All of the consoling and comforting that the nurse and I had tried had not helped, but Eduardo was very loving and patient. He knew just what to say to his little sister and she was soon calmed and coherent. Their mother did answer the third phone call and came to the school. Sandy was still quite upset and wanted to go home.

After this incident, she was too frightened of the playground noise and excitement to wait outside with the other children. Her classroom teacher met her each morning at the locked door and let her in early. There were several other falling incidences when she became hysterical. We knew to get her brother to calm her. Only one additional time did she have to leave school. Her comfort level at school, and her brother's help, allowed her to regain composure and return to her class after a brief stay with the nurse.

Sandy learned rather quickly, and while she had been behind in her grade level reading, her reading progressed until I had moved her to my group of grade five students, three girls, who were reading well. Over the course of the year I requested that she be tested for the "gifted" students program. The psychologist who did the testing with me found her to be in the exceptional range and she was a "double identified" special student. Her needs now were: physical therapy for walking, Gifted and Talented, and to continue in the learning disabilities program till her restaffing the next fall.

She was a delight to have in class. She had a very positive attitude about everything, even her own disability. The older girls loved her. We all read a middle school novel titled, "The Courage of Sarah Noble." This was a story about a young pioneer girl who was separated from her mother and other siblings. She and her father had gone on a journey to obtain supplies for the family, and their experience and great courage was well told in the short novel. All the girls were impressed with the information about the hardships of the pioneers, and the frightening experiences of the main character.

Since the girls had loved this story so, I bought a copy of the book for each of them at our school book fair. Sandy seemed the most appreciative. Shortly after this, Sandy's mother announced to us that her daughter would probably be a little anxious and have more problems, as there was a surgery scheduled. The doctors were going to operate on her legs to lengthen a tendon which they hoped would help her with mobility. The expectation was that she would then be able to walk more normally. Sandy was very worried and talked constantly about the impending operation. We discussed "courage" and I said to remember the courage of Sarah in the story. Her response was, "How about the courage of Sandy"? She had to endure two different scheduled times for her surgery because of conflicts with the operating physicians. When the time was finally set and surgery was really going to happen, her regular classroom members had taken up a collection and bought a gift and cards for Sandy. I did not know that they had gotten a teddy bear for her, and that is what I decided to buy to give her some comfort. She took both teddy bears to the hospital with her, and she and I named the one I bought for her, "Courage". Before she left for surgery we both said, "remember the Courage of Sandy."

The surgery went well and after a recovery time Sandy was back at school. She was now using a walker until she recovered more completely. Her legs appeared not so tight and it could be seen that her gait would be much improved. After some time, she was able to walk without her walker. Her gait was much improved, but was still a definite problem. Her mother said that there would be several additional surgeries over the next few years. Sandy said she would keep her bears with her.

The next reading for Sandy's reading group (now above their grade level testing) was the old novel that I had read at about the same age, as had *my* mother. We began reading the old favorite of numerous generations, "Anne of Green Gables." In conversation with the principal, I mentioned how well the group was reading and which book we had started. I had videos of the story and planned to use them so the girls could see the vintage clothing and sets. The principal told me that this book was her all time favorite from childhood, and she brought an "Anne of Green Gables" doll, that she had kept for years, to let the girls have in our room while we read the book.

The reading group loved finding new and unusual words and, rather than my just telling them the meanings, we would look them up in the dictionary. Often they were antiquated words that were not in the school's junior dictionary. One day they read in the book that the custodian for Anne's school took an apple from the teacher's desk, and Anne thought that he saw it as a "perquisite". We surely had to look up that word. I told the class that I doubted it was in our dictionary. It was! We laughed as they had all heard about "perks" on the job. I had not known of the derivation. I had been telling the girls that I would be retiring at the end of the year. They all thought that I should have my computer as a perquisite. Then they began finding other things that I should take. I shared this with the principal. She was not terribly amused.

The next year, as I was retired, I returned to school as a volunteer and worked with the "Gifted and Talented" program. I taught the students creative writing and was able to have a number of them published in a national poetry anthology. I continue volunteering in this endeavor at the time of this writing. I had Sandy in my group the first year, and she had one of her poems published. I've often wished that I had the "courage of Sandy".

The Vale Brothers

One of the nice things about teaching in the same school for a number of years, is that you get to know and teach brothers and sisters, and sometimes even children of your former students. In my school I had the good experience of dealing with three brothers over a period of several years. Each one of them was different. They all had perceptual problems that qualified them for special help in my program, but their personalities were extremely different. I, of course, became well acquainted with their mother who is a very lovely lady. I went to two of their high school graduations and a wedding for one of the boys. I only have daughters and I was impressed with the difference in raising only boys. Sarah, their mother, was single shortly after I met her and she was extremely devoted to her sons, and worked hard to support them over the years. She had very few close relatives to help her in her efforts, or to even be emotionally supportive. She worked in a factory and was on a production line, so she was on her feet for long hours at work. She would come home and take care of the boys, the dinner, and the house at night. It was a number of years before the boys were old enough to be of any great help with yard or house work. I really admired her efforts and the positive manner in which she raised her boys.

Climb a Tree

Warren was the oldest Vale Brother. He was in my class from grades two through five. He was a handsome young boy with sandy blond hair, large blue eyes, and a few freckles, on his impudent nose. He was very sociable and well liked by his peers. He was having problems learning to read. He worked intently and was very serious about school. He said he felt bad that he couldn't get good grades to please his mother and father, and hoped that they were not disappointed in him. Warren was scheduled with several other students from his grade. We had very pleasant instructional periods and he was working very hard.

A few months after start of school, it appeared that Warren was preoccupied. He seemed a little sad and not as well focused. He had talked a lot about his father, and how his father was from England. He shared stories that his father told him about growing up in England. He talked about the food, entertainment, and schools there. His classmates were interested and asked him lots of questions that he in turn asked his father, and he then reported the information back to us. Warren was not talking much now about his dad. One day he said, "I'm sad, my dad is not feeling well. He has been sick for quite a while". After this, he often remarked about how his dad was no longer working, how he was not feeling well, and issued concern about the fact that he was not seeming to get better.

As the weeks went by, we heard more and more concern about Warren's dad not being well. Then, finally, Warren was not just sad or preoccupied, he was very upset. He said to me, "I think my dad is dying." When I asked him why he felt that way he responded, "I heard him talking on the phone to his friend. He was saying he was tired of feeling so sick all the time, that he wished he could just die NOW and get it all over with." I was alarmed and decided to call his mother, Sarah, and let her know what Warren had said so she could relieve him of any unnecessary worry. It turned out that his father had cancer, and *was* dying. Sarah was glad that I had called her as she and her husband had not shared this information with Warren and Scott, her two boys. Sarah was now pregnant with her third son.

Scott was too young to have this information, but Sarah took Warren aside and talked with him about the illness.

Concerns about his father's health continued to worry Warren. He talked about it from time to time with me and his classmates. He had stopped telling us stories about England. I knew that his dad was getting progressively sicker and supposed that he was not having the great conversations about his former country with his son. Warren was working well but not with the enthusiasm that he had shown earlier. His academics were not as important to him now. Soon we heard that his father had been hospitalized and was very weak.

One Sunday morning I got a call from Sarah. She said that she was at the hospital with Warren and that his father had just passed away. I issued my condolences and asked if there were anything that I could do. "Yes," she replied, "Would you please talk with Warren? I am so sorry to call you on the weekend, but Warren is very upset. I asked him if he had anyone that he would like to talk to and he asked me if we could call you". I was very flattered that Warren wanted to tell me about it. He came to the phone and we talked for a little while. I asked him if he knew of anything that he could do that might make him feel better. He had a strange response. He said that he would really like to go climb a tree and go as high as he could. I told him that sounded like a good idea and that he should go and do it. He said he was concerned that his mother would not understand why he would want to climb a tree, and asked if I would please talk to her and explain that the climbing would make him feel better, and that he was not just "playing around". He put his mother back on the phone and I told her that the feelings he got when he climbed would alleviate his deep sorrow, that the climbing would be a way for him to cope with his father's death. She said she understood, and Warren went to find the best tree where he could climb very high—up to the top.

The next years as I had Warren, I appreciated the extra effort, and real trials that Sarah endured in raising her boys alone. John, her baby, was born and Scott had started school.

A Model Student

Scott had learning problems like his older brother. Warren was in middle school and doing well. I was pleased to have Scott in my group. Scott had very light blonde hair and was all boy. He was friendly, and very cooperative. One of the easiest students to teach that I had encountered. Scott was in a group with a girl and one other boy who had autism, I was experimenting with using story writing to teach language and spelling. I wanted there to be a lot of social interaction to help my autistic student. Scott was perfect for the task of socializing Travis. The girl, Chris, had some problems with self-confidence. Scott was a good influence on both of them. The book was a cooperative venture for the three of them. It turned out to be a very charming story that the kids wrote themselves into. When it came to illustrating the book, Scott proved to be a very good artist. He drew several pages of illustrations that included buildings. He drew buildings with accurate perspective and he had not had any lessons in this skill. Scott said that he would like to be an architect when he grew up, or maybe just build houses. He said he wanted to drive a big red truck like his father's, get married, and have three kids. Scott was a strong young boy and I thought he seemed like a potentially perfect redneck,. I envisioned him working on houses, driving his truck accompanied by his wife, and kids and a dog hanging out the windows. Scott was very sensitive and accepting of others. This was why he did such a fine job in helping with the autistic child.

He became one of my most favorite students in my career. I had the pleasure of teaching Scott from grade three through grade five. He still retained difficulties with his academics throughout his school years. He seemed so perceptive and so understanding of his classmates, and even adults. One day he related to me that he thought that his fifth grade teacher was angry at her husband for having a stroke. I asked him what made him think that. He said that he could see it in her face. He said that she didn't like having to work while her husband was staying at home, and that she didn't like doing everything for him when she came home. He said the teacher had brought her husband to school and the husband was showing how he could hit the golf balls even with his compromised physical skills. Scott said that the way that she talked about him at different times, and her remarks about her returning to teaching, after having been able to stay at home, made him believe that she was really angry underneath. I had already given this some thought, as I had heard her various conversations and remarks about her family in our teachers' lounge. His teacher was married to a Christian denominational preacher. From her reports, she loved being a minister's wife and helping the needy in her church. She had let me know that "her church" invited all the single people to a special Thanksgiving dinner, even the divorcees (of which I was one!). This had seemed rather bigoted to me. She did seem upset that her husband could no longer serve as their minister. He did give a sermon or two on occasion, but he was retired and was no longer paid. Her remarks did express distaste at having to again become a teacher. I repositioned my future vision of Scott as the redneck, and placed him as a learned psychoanalyst with fantastic insight. Scott seemed to be very wise beyond his years.

Scott moved on to middle school and still came to my school on occasion, just to visit. He would go see all of his past teachers, who also admired what a fine person Scott was. Scott told me of concerns about his younger brother who would soon be in my program. Sarah was having difficulties with John in his daycare situation.

Scott came to visit many times when in high school. He was not adjusting well at that level, and when he came to visit a few times in the middle of the day, I was suspicious. He had said that he was out of school as the teachers were having meetings, or gave me other excuses. It seems that things got so hard for him that he had dropped out. Within a few months, Sarah managed to get him enrolled in the local alternative high school. He did much better but did not complete the program and get his degree. Now I needed to revisit the redneck possibility.

I'm Not So Bad

Meanwhile John had become my student. John was a darling second grader who could not say his R's. He worked with both me and the speech therapist. John was a handful. He did not always tell the truth and was not so nearly academically inclined as either brother. Warren had gone on to college but had dropped out after the first year. It seemed that he was prone to going to lots of parties and really enjoying the college life. He had gotten drunk at a party and had fallen through a glass door and severely injured his leg. This took him out of school. Sarah had thought the absence was temporary and kept encouraging him to return. He did return for one more year.

Scott had told me that John had problems with honesty. He said that the babysitter had noticed money missing from her purse. When it happened a second time, she made the determination that it was John and refused to babysit him anymore. Sarah was left with finding a new sitter. John denied taking the money, but was more careful with the next sitter.

Scott had been quite small when his father died. He did tell of times when he remembered handing his dad a can of pop when they sat outside on the patio. He was very respectful of his mother and told me how proud he was of her. He said she worked hard and did not "date" or go out a lot, as she was so dedicated to taking care of him and his brothers. One day, Scott came by while he was still in high school. He was upset and angry with John. Their mother was distressed about losing her wedding rings. She had taken them off and put them on the headboard of her bed. They were gone and she had taken the bed apart, cleaned the room thoroughly, and still had not found them. Scott told me that he feared that John had found them. He asked me to try and find out.

I dismissed the other students, who were in John's group, a little early. This gave me some time to talk with John privately. I brought up the subject of his mother's rings. I let him know that Scott had told me how very upset their mother was. John remarked that she really was upset. I talked to him about his dad, about how his mother had suffered with his illness and death, and how very important it was to her to have the rings to remember his father by. He agreed. I suggested that they must be in the house somewhere, as Sarah had last seen them when she took them off at night in her bed. He agreed. I suggested that it would be a wonderful thing if he and Scott, together, could search again and maybe find them. How pleased that would make his mom. He agreed again. They searched and the rings magically appeared under the bed—where I had told John that they might be. John never admitted to ever having seen them when they were lost.

John had become my good friend. He told a few of his fifth grade buddies that I was his grandmother. One day after school he came to talk to me, accompanied by two of his friends. They asked if I were *really* John's grandmother. I told them that it surely felt that way, as I had been friends with his family for a long time, and I told them, smiling, that I was John's adopted grandmother.

John advanced to middle school, still needing assistance in special programs. He was a bit of a handful there. He had some lying, some truancy, and Scott was still coming to visit and telling me of John's misdeeds. John came back to our school to visit many times after school and had complaints about hard it was in middle school. He was losing his "w" sound for his "r", growing taller and acting much more mature.

My school staff and the middle school staff started working on helping students adjust from elementary to middle school. The L.D. teacher at the middle school began the tradition of coming to our school and conferring about the special education students that would be attending her middle school. She was accompanied by her school counselor. I invited the fifth grade teachers. We had good communication and they took notes that would help them in working with the new sixth graders when they arrived. The counselor from middle school asked me about John. She said she knew that he had been in my class for several years. She said, "Are you really his grandmother?" I told her about our true relationship. She said that she was not surprised. There were lots of problems with John and the counselor had asked John if he had someone with whom he could talk to, about his school academic and discipline problems. He had said, "Yes, my grandmother, she works at my old elementary school." Then John had given her my name. I was upset with John's lying but glad that he felt he could talk with me.

John's mother, Sarah, did not date or go out often all the time the boys were growing up. She was working so hard and the parenting kept her busy. As they got older, Warren gone from home, Scott much older, and John also becoming a young man, childcare was no longer a problem. Sarah began going to the Elk's club after work with some of her co-workers. She met a wonderful man about her age and they were very compatible. He was a brick layer and worked hard. He loved gardening, as did Sarah. He did many fix-it things around the house. In exchange for my counseling with John about his school problems, Sarah's new friend came and repaired the stone work around my flowerbed. It had been crumbled by a car running into it. Sarah and Jim were married and Jim seemed to be a big help with the boys.

John did come and talk often. Scott had now dropped out of school. His mother was very concerned about his lengthy absences from home. John came to visit one afternoon and had some exciting news. He was agitated but somewhat happy. He reported that he was not so bad anymore, that Scott had upset his mother much more than he ever had. He would not tell me what Scott had done. I supposed that he was into drugs, stealing, or something equally serious. John seemed relieved that Scott was now a bigger problem than he. He repeated his joy in this development in his subsequent visits. I had not heard from Scott for a while and worried about what he could be involved in. John was very coy and made some remarks that intimated that it was a sexual situation. I had asked if he had been in trouble with the law. John denied that there were any law breaking problems. I had just about come to the conclusion that Scott had encountered a sexual identity problem.

I called Sarah and talked with her for a while. I let her know that John had told me that Scott was having some difficulties. She acknowledged that he was and that it was serious. I asked her if she would like me to talk with him. She said yes, but that she did not believe that he would tell me what his problems were. I told her what I suspected, and she said I was correct. Scott had started working in a fast food stand at the mall. There was an older gay man who was working with him, he and Scott had become friends. Sarah had talked with him many times, spent hours crying over the problem, even had her husband, Jim, try to talk with Scott. The whole family was having much difficulty adjusting to Scott's new inclinations. She said that Scott was there but that he would probably not reveal what was going on. She was correct. He talked with me, said there were some problems with his family situation, but did not divulge his relationship with the man involved. He just said his mom did not like his personal decisions.

Scott came to visit me some time later. I had heard that his "companion" (they were now living together) was very controlling and abusive to Scott. His friend had a car and he provided their residence. They lived in an area that was somewhat remote. Scott had no money as he did not work. His friend had the car and the money, so Scott was trapped at home. The relationship was becoming hostile. I told Scott that I felt he deserved to be treated better and that the situation did not seem workable for him. Several months later John came and told me that the relationship had gotten violent and that he, John, and his other brother, Warren, had gone to Scott's home and helped him to pack and leave the house. Scott lived at home with his mother for a short time, and then developed a more positive relationship with another male.

Scott is still with that companion. They have a home in a suburb and are caring for several severely retarded men. Scott is so compassionate that I am sure the care is good. Sarah, the step-father, Warren, and John have adjusted to Scott's life-style. Scott and his companion were both in Sarah's home for Christmas. Warren was married, divorced, and has a new girl friend. John has been living in another state and calls me long distance from time to time. The boys called me last Christmas time from Sarah's, I spoke with all three of them. Sarah calls me "their grandmother" and writes me notes and sends pictures. I have a picture of my three "grandsons" on my dresser. Sarah had asked me often when I thought I might retire. I told her I could not do that until all the Vales Boys were out of school. I made true my vow. I am now retired.

Not My Flag

Julio had recently come from Mexico. He was in second grade and could not read at all. He was a small boy with straight dark hair that he would flip by tossing his head. He was totally disinterested in reading. He could do his math and it was up to grade level. Julio was great at art. He looked forward to his free time on Friday so that he could draw. He was remarkable in his approach. He drew objects with their details first and then the main form at the end. He made a box or french fries with all the individual fries, then the box. He had just the ends of the fries drawn that would be seen with their positions in the box. He drew a couch with the tufts and buttons first and then the actual couch. It seemed that he must have a complete visual picture in his head and approached the details first. I had been in art school in college and had *never* seen an approach like this.

Art was very important to Julio. He often drew the flag of Mexico in great detail, making beautiful renditions of it. When the group stood to say the Pledge of Allegiance, Julio refused. He said that is *not* my flag and would then draw another picture of *his* flag. Because of Julio's artistic ability, I altered his reading instruction. He had not been able to even remember letters or sound of letters and he had no sight words he could recall. I started using my drawings of words and then Julio's drawings to help him learn complete words. It was working. We made a small book with words that he was learning, and that told a simple little story. We had a tiny book about a mad cat. Julio had made the cat look very mad. We moved on to some Dr. Seus's stories, which worked quite well. Julio needed the "sight word" approach and phonics did him little or no good. As his reading vocabulary increased, I bought some comic books that Julio loved. I would help him with words he did not know. As he reread them a number of times, he added more and more words to his vocabulary. He was finally enjoying reading.

I showed some of Julio's art work to our art teacher and she had him do some pictures, that she used for an art show that would be put up in the local mall. Julio still insisted that he loved the Mexican flag, and that he was going back there soon. I wonder if he did as he did moved away and we never heard from him. If he had entered another school in the district, we would have sent his records on. Even if he had entered another school somewhere else in our state, records would have been requested. I fancy that Julio is now some great artist in his beloved Mexico.

Rainbow Dreams

Elizabeth was a bubbly, round faced kindergartener with some learning problems. She had sandy blonde, and very fine, wispy hair, large blue eyes, and a sprinkle of freckles across her perky little nose. Her teachers, family, and friends all called her Lizzy. She called herself "Yizzy" as she was having speech problems, along with being behind in beginning academic skills. Lizzy was staffed into my program and we were working on learning colors, letters, numerals, and such to prepare Lizzy for grade one. Lizzy came down two long hallways to my classroom every morning at 10:00.

She worked hard on learning her colors and would repeat my words of "yellow like the sun" as, "lellow like the sun." Often she would forget which color went with sun, sky, grass, clouds, and rose. We could get "green like the sky" and "red, like the sun" at the beginning, but it finally worked out alright. She was counting well, and could name her geometric shapes correctly. As we moved to letters, I had gotten some Sesame Street tapes to enhance the instruction. One tape, with which we spent a lot of time, was for the letter, "L". On the tape the character would sing, "La, la, la, Lollipop." and Lizzy would copy with "Ya, ya, ya, ya, yoyipop". I put her name into the exercise and she sang, "Ya, ya, ya, ya, Yizzy". All of her other letters were easier and she could name and identify them with their sounds. We worked endlessly on the "L" and I kept trying to make some time with her speech therapist for guidelines. Finally, I decided to figure out some help for myself. I had shown Lizzy how to hold her mouth but had not realized that the tongue position was so important. In mouthing the word for myself I figured out what to tell Lizzy. I had her place her tongue on the roof of her mouth and try one more time. It worked! We were both excited and I escorted her to her room, and had Lizzy tell her teacher her name. She proudly said, "Lizzy". Her teacher responded happily.

After a few days of her saying her letter "L" correctly, she announced that since she was "so grownup that she could say her "L's", she thought she should be called Elizabeth. Elizabeth, she was then for the rest of the time that she was in my program. Her teacher, mother, and classmates all honored her request to be "Elizabeth".

Elizabeth had seven brothers and her parents were delighted to finally have an adorable little girl. She told me with great pride and expectation that she wanted to be a singer when she grew up. She said she spent time listening and singing with the country singers on her dad's tapes. Her dad was an auto mechanic, as were her two much older brothers. It was easy to conceive of Elizabeth, grown up and singing country western songs before a mic. She had a perfect personality for it.

Because of her morning schedule with me, there were often opportunities for her to remain for additional time during the day to attend assemblies that were later, and she, with her mom's permission, would stay for lunch with me, and then attend the first grade class for the assembly. One day I asked her if she would like to stay. I always told her what the performance would be and she could choose to stay or go home. She seemed puzzled and unable to decide, this was more than her normal hesitation. She told me how hard it was to make a choice as she did not have her cat there to help her. She said she would ask the cat about things and tell it the pros and cons and he would help her make a good decision. She said, "This side of my head says, 'Yes, yes,

yes'. But this side says,'No, no, no'". I told her she could tell me all of the reasons for and against—maybe that would help. It did, she made the choice to stay.

Another day Elizabeth was not her usual sunny self and seemed distracted and sad. I asked her if she were upset about something. Her response was, "I had a dream, it was not too bad, but it was not happy, and I did not see the rainbow at the end." It seemed that whenever Elizabeth had dreams, at the very end a rainbow would appear in the sky above. She said it had always happened, but not this day. I told her how very lucky she was to have such a blessing, and that I had never known anyone who had rainbows for the end of their dreams.

Elizabeth learned well and was more than ready for grade one. At the end of the school year I had "staffed" Elizabeth out of my special program. I watched her grow and move to middle school. She was a delight. When telling her good-bye as she moved on to another school, I told her I would surely remember her and asked her if she could guess *how* I would remember her. "Yes", she said with a big smile, "You will remember me as the girl who had rainbows for the end of my dreams". Elizabeth is grown, married now with several children. I don't think she made good her promise to be a country western singer, but I suspect that there are still rainbows in her dreams.

Bounty Hunter

A new family moved into our school attendance zone. Three of the older children were in school, a teenage girl in the middle school, a girl in grade five and brother in grade four. The grade five girl, Gina, was a good student, responsible and academically focused. Her younger brother was a real handful. He had a charming personality, was clever, and up to much mischief. He also had been diagnosed in his prior school as having learning disabilities. So, Lawrence was scheduled into my program. I enjoyed him from the start. He always had a very interesting outlook on everything. He was a class clown and continually disrupted his regular class. He had less audience in my smaller class but kept us all amused with his wittiness and clever comments. One of Lawrence's first interactions with me was to remark that I should not be single. He had asked, and I had said I was divorced and raising two children. He was concerned that this situation had lasted too long and that I should remarry. I told him that my prince had not come riding up on his white horse, as yet, but I was waiting.

Lawrence was a constant concern with behavioral problems and silliness in his classroom. But even the teachers who dealt with him had to admit that he had a great sense of humor and was a great distraction. On one occasion, he came to stand by me at our classroom door. A classroom was passing in the hallway and the children all scrambled and scurried trying to get something from the floor. "Did you do something?" I asked of Lawrence. I got his usual "Who me?" look and no admission. This happened several other times, I never did see what had caused the confusion in the hallway. One day, I was in the hall and perceived the scurrying from a different angle. Lawrence was surely throwing something out onto the hall floor. When I asked him what he had tossed out there, he acted embarrassed at being caught, and then looked self-consciously guilty. "It's just change" he replied with a coy smile. I asked him why he would throw money out into the hall. He responded that he just liked to see them all scramble to get it. Just then another class went by and we were still by the doorway. "See?" said Lawrence, tossing a few more coins, "They all fight over who is going to get it. I like to watch it." When I told him it was rather silly to throw away his money in that fashion, he smiled and shook his head. "It's just like the rich giving to the poor" he said laughing. The teachers leading their classes down the hallway seemed confused about the commotion. None of the kids had reported money being thrown to them. I did ask that he not disturb the classes in the hallway in that way anymore. He complied, but I know he found other entertainment of similar worth.

After summer break, Lawrence returned—still a lively spirit. He seriously asked me if my prince had come during the summer. I told him that at one point I thought he had, but I had been mistaken. I really didn't know where the rascal was hiding. One day Lawrence came in with a picture he had drawn. He had exceptional artistic talent that had been noticed by both the art teacher and his classroom teachers. Lawrence's picture depicted a scruffy looking vagabond on a horse. The man had a beard with a spider in it. He had socks drawn with holes in the heels and wiggly marks indicating smell emitting from the shoeless feet. The drawing was of a desert with the horseman and an old lady sitting on a rocking chair. She was skinny with knobby knees and also quite disheveled looking. The balloon above her said, "Oh, my pince (Lawrence's spelling was not good), where have you been?" Above the prince were the words "I got caught in the swamp". Lawrence's class time was shared with two other fifth grade students. One of the other boys had a divorced mother. When I said to Lawrence "If that is my prince, I am going to tell him to ride on by." Lawrence's classmate said, "My mom don't want him either". In addition to the beard, the holey socks, and the bad smell indications, The prince had very wild hair and a bird sitting in it.

When we were having free time and lots of communication, we all discussed Lawrence's prince drawing. I told him that there were lots of single ladies around and, if there were a swamp with a prince caught in it, Lawrence might do well to go dredge the swamp and charge a bounty fee. I told him I had a single sister, several single friends, his classmate's mother, all who needed a prince, and I was sure this could be a lucrative business. Maybe there were lots of lost princes in that swamp. Lawrence and his friends enjoyed this silly exchange. I soon forgot about the prince and our conversation

Some many weeks later, Lawrence came to school with an obviously home made patch over one eye. After parent conferences and further knowledge about his home situation, I was concerned for his safety. He had a stepfather whom, he had said, threw him down the stairs. There were remarks from his mother about problems at home, and Lawrence had said several times that he hated his stepfather and wished that his mother had not remarried. His own father had died a number of years earlier. His father and mother had three children. The stepfather and his mother had an additional two girls (now in grades one and two) and a boy that was not yet in school. I asked several time about his eye. Was it hurting? Yes, kind of. Had he hit it—was it injured? No, not really.

Well, what was wrong with it? I told him that we needed to go to the nurse and have her look at it. He was more than reluctant. Since I felt obligated to have his injury inspected I insisted we go to the nurse's office. I went with him. He acted embarrassed and very uncomfortable, adding to my concern that he was concealing an injury. The nurse had him remove his patch. His eye was red and seemed a little irritated but the nurse could see nothing wrong. She advised that he keep the patch off, and perhaps she would look at it again later. Lawrence and I started back down the hall to my classroom. He shuffled as he walked and then said softly,

"Docky, you shouldn't have made me do that!"

"Why, Lawrence? I was concerned about your eye."

"It's okay", he said impatiently, "I was just being a bounty hunter".

I guess this was akin to throwing the coins to the poor.

Lawrence was more than entertaining the rest of the year. He grew much physically and academically. He entered middle school the next year, as a tall and average functioning sixth grader.

I became good friends with Lawrence's mom, and later I had two of Lawrence's siblings in my class. After Lawrence entered middle school and had been there almost a year, he came to visit. He was very concerned. He told me that "they" were going to put him in an emotionally disturbed class. When I questioned why he thought this, he said they told him and his mom that his behavior was disruptive, and that if it did not improve he might be considered for that special class. I asked Lawrence to tell me what kind of behavior he was exhibiting. He only shrugged his shoulders and smiled. I told him that he must be doing something that upset his teachers, and asked if he could think of anything. He got a large smile on his face and reported the following episode.

"It was a warm day, the windows were all open. I was just bored. I started making rather quiet little bird sounds with my mouth. I can make lots of different bird sounds. The teacher looked very concerned. I thought it was funny, She didn't seem to know where they were coming from. I didn't move my mouth much. I made more, and some more different ones. She seemed upset and went over and closed the window.

I think she thought that would stop the "bird noise". I kept doing it. Later a kid told on me."

I told Lawrence that if he kept up the distractions that he would be put in the special class. I told him that I had taught in one such class, and I did not believe that he would like being in it. I told him the boys where I taught were very disturbed. I said that he was not disturbed, that he could control his behavior, and if he acted "crazy", continued to upset teachers and classrooms, that they would surely be justified in placing him in that setting. Lawrence decided to control his behavior, at least in the classroom. He was able to stay in the regular programs and finally graduated.

About a year after he graduated, Lawrence wanted to join the military. He told me that he had taken a test for admission to the marines and had not passed it. He did not do well in the language portion of the test. He said his vocabulary score was too low. He asked if I could help him learn more words and then he would retake the test, or test in a different area of military service. We had sessions of language tutoring for a few months. I made silly pictures to illustrate word meanings for Lawrence. He was making good progress, but got a different job and lost interest in the future retesting. I did not see him again for a long time, although I was in frequent contact with his mother.

Over the years I had two of Lawrence's siblings. a sister and a brother. Both of them had learning disabilities. Reports of Lawrence were good, then bad. He had decided not to help much around the house. He was still living at home. He had helped his mother (now divorced), with the younger children, mowing the lawn, helping with cooking, and so forth. He stopped helping with anything at home. He was becoming a problem as he was associating with some unemployed and rather lazy friends who sat about and did nothing. His mother asked him to move out. He later got a job, dropped his bad connections and did very well. Lawrence was large, handsome and rather muscular. He started body building and was "Mr. Colorado" on the cover of a body-building magazine. He told me that he was offered a contract if he would take steroids, he refused. I was very proud of him. Then I was later told by his mother that he was the maintenance chief for a large gated condominium complex. A number of years ago he began work on a cruise ship, I do not know in what capacity, but he surely has great social skills for entertainment and making others feel happy and accepted. At the time of this writing Lawrence is still working for a large cruise ship company.

Being Normal

A number of years after I had been working with this program, a mother came to talk to me about her son who would be coming into my program. She wanted me to know about autism. I let her know that when I had worked at the university, I had been involved as the supervisor of several student teachers who were spending their training periods in autistic programs, and that I had studied much about autism, and had observed a number of different settings in the metropolitan area for autism. She gave me a book to read by the now famous Temple Grandin, who overcame her disability of autism and had written her experience in dealing with the problem. The mother and father of the student I would be helping had genetic counseling after their son, Travis, had been born. He was their first child and they decided not to have others, as autism might be a genetic problem.

Travis was an attractive fourth grader. He had thick blonde hair and large brown eyes, that seldom made contact with others. He was tall and well built for his age. I put Travis in a class with two other fourth grade students. They were all working on language and reading skills. When I first started working with Travis he rarely looked at me. I would see him in the hallway, passing with his class in a line, and he never looked up. I started reaching over and touching his arm or shoulder and speaking to him. When I touched him he would look at me. After a while he not only spoke but looked at me in the hallway before I touched him. He was also improving in the classroom. He was more apt to talk with the other two students there and was completing more of his work.

Initially, Travis would work on his language skills for a while and then stop, just staring into space. I would ask him what he was thinking and direct him to return to his writing. I looked up from my instruction with the others in the group and refocused Travis often. I asked him what he was thinking. He said, "Nothing, I'm just on level three of my game". I never understood why his mother, who had so much information about autism, would allow him to spend the amount of time he reportedly did on video games. Repetitive motions are usually discouraged for autistic children and I would assume that connections to a game, rather than persons or reality, is not good for helping autistic behaviors. After this announcement from Travis, I would call his name and say, "Travis, come back to *this* level". He would smile and return to his writing. Soon I would only snap my fingers and he would "come back".

I decided to involve all three students in a project that we could all work on together. This was mostly to help Travis with socialization. All three were only slightly below grade level and could benefit from regular spelling and reading sessions, and then we would spend two days of the week writing a book. They wanted to write about children who "lived" in our school. We talked about how comfortable our room was and they said it would be fun to live there. I took them on a walk past the kitchen and showed them an old shower room, used many years earlier. I showed them the basement door and told them the furnace to heat the school was down those stairs.

The children in their book lived in the future, and the school (our school) had long been closed. The children lived in an orphanage where they were treated cruelly. They escaped and came to the old abandoned school. On the playground they found an old dinosaur egg that they took into the old unlocked school. They put the egg in the oven in the kitchen and hatched it. The dinosaur lived with the children in the abandoned school. They had many activities with their new pet and he helped them to get along in the school. They were able to connect the gas and electricity. They found money, and the dinosaur flew them to the local super market where they bought food, clothing, and roller skates. They skated for hours down the long school halls. The real children each named and described one of the three children in the book. They would take turns telling various parts of the story. I would write it all down, type and copy it for their editing. They illustrated the pages. This exercise was great for Travis. He would often get off topic or present something too fantastic for this story, and the others would call him back to the story and ask him to change his ideas if they did not fit. The other two children loved the experience and when I would see them years later they would talk about our book. I still have the story and I think that someday I may publish it as a child's book.

Travis was becoming more and more normal in his social skills and his attention level. The next year when he was in grade five, he developed a crush on a pretty classmate. He secretly told me about it and said he wanted to become more normal, as he liked this girl, wanted her to like him, and was going to go to middle school next year. I made a little card for Travis that he put in his pant's pocket for easy reference. I took the word "normal" and used each letter to remind him of some normal social skills for him to attain. The skills were to make eye contact, stay on task, keep to the topic in conversations, and I cannot remember the other two we had. Travis worked very hard on the skills and was appearing and acting more and more like a regular fifth grader. He was also included more and more in playground and regular classroom activities.

His mother came to the fifth grade graduation and said how pleased she was with Travis' progress. I spoke with her several times after he went to middle school and learned he had a very good adjustment there and seemed to be doing well. He would be a grown man now and I do not know how life turned out for him. I believe that he continued to work on "being normal" and is probably enjoying a good life.

Young Tutor

Several years after Lawrence (the bounty hunter) left for middle school, I was privileged to have his little half-sister, Maria, in my program. Just as Lawrence was hard to manage, eager to upset the system, and a mischief maker, Maria was the complete opposite. She was shy, reticent to say too much, and extremely cooperative. Maria was reading below her grade level and was diagnosed with learning disabilities. Often children in the same family will experience the same visual perceptual problems. I had three of Minnie's children in my program. Minnie was Lawrence's and Maria's lovely mother. Minnie was a stay-at-home mom but she worked very hard. She developed a fantastic recipe for the most heavenly cinnamon rolls that ever were made. She was known by the mayor's office staff who bought her rolls, by a number of other schools for whom she baked, and many businesses in the city. Minnie would deliver her rolls to the various offices, and was kept very busy baking several times a week. A local supermarket offered her money to use her recipe and give her credit, but she refused. The mayor's office came up with some plans to help her start her own business with a shop in the downtown area. She again refused. She had seven children and a husband to care for, and desired to stay in her home and do her baking. Her husband was in the military and she needed to supplement the family income.

Maria was making good progress in her language skills. Her reading was improving and she was overcoming some of the extreme shyness that she first exhibited. She was very affectionate and loving and especially good with small children. Because of her learning style she needed to repeat words and reread to impress the words on her mind. She was reading at a first grade level and loved to reread her stories. To help her and several younger students, I assigned her to a group where she could act as a tutor and help the younger ones to read the stories that she had already read. Her teaching improved her knowledge and her self confidence. Maria said many times that she would love to be a teacher when she grew up.

Her mother, Minnie, had been married before and had three children. Those children did not care much for their stepfather and Lawrence had considerable problems in dealing with his harsh discipline. Minnie was pregnant with her last child and things were not going well at home. Because of my earlier involvement with Lawrence, Minnie and I had become good friends. We often spent long periods on the telephone late at night. Minnie and I shared lots of our problems. Her husband was unaware of our friendship. Lawrence and his father were having more difficulties and Minnie and her husband were experiencing some marital problems. Her husband was very deceitful and was not very honest with Minnie about his activities. He came to back-to-school night and conferred with me about Maria. Minnie had not been feeling well and he had offered to do the parent conferences. I mentioned that I knew Maria's mother was working with her to help her with her reading. He paused with an odd expression on his face and then very seriously said, "My wife is pregnant and she has been having some difficulties. She has not been herself." I was surprised and asked what the problem might be. "Well," he said, "since her pregnancy she just is not wrapped too tight", implying that Minnie was a bit out of it. I remarked that I was very surprised as she seemed quite fine when I spoke with her, just yesterday. I guess I sounded a little annoyed as he discontinued any further remarks.

Soon after this there was a big upset at home over some actions of Maria's father and he left the home. Minnie was now a single mother but the divorce was further down the road. Poor Maria was devastated. Unlike her half-siblings, Maria loved her father. She went into a real slump. Her academics suffered and she was very unhappy all the time. Minnie was apprised of this, but she had a lot to deal with handling her own discomforts. Maria was already a little heavy for a third grader and she began gaining even more weight. She also started a strange habit of sucking her tongue. I had only seen this behavior in the severely retarded children. Maria continued being very sad and not focusing on her school work.

Children in the special eduction programs were required to have an annual review. At this time they were given academic tests to assess their academic skills. Every three years they were also given an intellectual test. If they still qualified under the state and federal guidelines for the handicapped, they were retained in the program. It was suggested that Maria, because of her depression, tongue sucking, and very slow appearance and actions, be given an intellectual test. Maria had an average I.Q. in her initial testing but she was behaving very much as a retarded child. The new testing indicated that this was the case. Her

I.Q. had dramatically dropped. Before our formal conference, I asked the head psychologist in the district, with whom I had an excellent relationship, if he would come and give Maria additional testing. After discussing her case, he agreed to do so. The further testing placed her not quite so low, but in a borderline area. This psychologist attended the staffing conference and attested to the fact that she was having much distress over the loss of her father, and that traumatic situations in children's lives could certainly affect the I.Q. scores. From his testing and conferring with Maria he was sure that she was not retarded. She remained in my program.

One day the very unfriendly teacher who worked down the hall from me, noticed this psychologist in the school office. She marched right up to him and demanded that he should place Maria in the retarded program because, as she said, "She IS retarded". I was also present in the office area as she made her demand. I was so proud of him as he responded with, "I could NOT place her in a retarded program, as she is certainly NOT retarded." He thanked her for her concern and said that she was unaware of our specific guidelines for the various programs. She was angry and deflated. I did not know why she was so negative toward Maria, the child was in her grade level but not in *her* classroom.

Maria became a strong independent reader before she left for middle school. She remained in special classes throughout middle school. In high school she was in regular classes. She did a work-study program in the high school and was an office assistant. She loved school, loved learning, and still would remark that one day she would be a teacher. In her last years in high school she took classes in early childhood development from the community college. She received special recognition for her work in this area at her high school graduation. Maria did not go on to be a teacher. She worked in the private sector for a few years in a very impressive position. The last information that I had was that she was married, her husband has served several years in Iraq, is now home and they are trying to start a family. I strongly believe that Maria will be as wonderful a mother as is Minnie. Minnie and her husband were divorced and a number of years later he came back into the area desiring to be involved in his children's lives. He was very apologetic to Minnie for his past actions. He had developed a severe illness, but did become close to his children. He has recently died and Minnie was at his side during his severe illness and death.

Names

Never have I seen such a cool, sophisticated fourth grader. He had an adult swagger and was able to handle any situation. Chance did have a learning disability but that did not seem to affect his self-esteem. He was so cool that all the kids looked up to him, and even the teachers treated him with dignity. After I had developed a good relationship with him, I would tease Chance about his name. Often I would tell him this is your "last chance, Chance." He accepted my remarks well, until one day when he was a little out of sorts. He said, "I am very lucky to have this name. I am very lucky my parents did not just call me 'Boy' as that is more like them. We have a cat named 'Cat' and a dog just called 'Dog'". Chance was a hard worker and was destined not to remain in my program for long. That was sad as he was such an asset. Kids would not be teased about a special class that Chance chanced to be in. Chance had a wonderful sense of humor and always had a joke or two to tell. He was delighted to let me know that his parents had gotten another cat and that they had named it "Phone Book". They were becoming quite creative with their naming. I really did like Chance's name. It sounded like a name for a country western singer or a rock star. I think it also assisted him with his positive self-esteem.

"Dog" ran away and Chance's family decided to get a new dog. Of all breeds to pick they got a huge Saint Bernard. The dog was from the pound and was not very well behaved. The family was having great difficulty in maintaining such a large misbehaving pet. It took them a while to find a proper name for him. and each day the students and I would ask how the "naming" was proceeding. After several weeks the new dog was still without a name. One day as Chance entered the room he said, "I have good news. The dog has a name." He would not divulge the name until the other members of his group arrived. The announcement was funny and Chance knew he needed everyone there for his proclamation. "The dog's name," he said very dramatically, "is… Norton Frickey and Associates." We were all quite amused and surprised at the selection. This was the name of a local legal firm, that dealt with accident cases. Everyone was acquainted with the name as it was so often on television ads.

Almost daily we would ask Chance about Norton Frickey and Associates. One had to use the entire name as that was what was so humorous. The dog did not adjust well to the family, nor did the family adjust well to the dog. It seemed that he got into a different bit of mischief almost every day. Norton Frickey and Associates ate everything, or at least chewed it. Chance's parents became more and more annoyed with the destruction.

The final straw came after a long weekend. The family was trying to have a barbeque with some friends in the back yard. It seems that Norton Frickey and Associates had been there first and chewed up the patio furniture. This had all but ruined the weekend. Chance's mother said that she was ready to give up. Chance was rightfully worried as when he arrived in the middle of the week he was very low spirited, unusual for Chance. When we asked about his dog he was quite upset. "I no longer have him," he said sadly, "We took Norton Frickey and Associates to the Dumb Friends League." We were all sad. We were sad for Chance's loss, sad for Norton, and sad that our entertainment was gone.

Months later, I was at a restaurant with a family member and a couple of friends. The husband was a lawyer and I started to relate my story of the infamous dog. "Oh," my friend said, "I know Norton Frickey well, we have worked together a number of times." I was a little embarrassed but responded with, "Well, when you see him again let him know that somewhere in heaven there is a dog named after his law firm." I was fairly sure that Norton had not been adoptable and had been "put down". And as we all know, all dogs go to heaven. I have often wondered that, if Chance married and had children, what he might have named his kids.

An Over Achiever?

Early in my years with the learning disabled kids, I had a lovely second grader named Paula. She was behind in her language skills and a little low in reading. She was very bright and had a severe visual perceptual problem. She also was somewhat hyperactive, which was unusual for a girl. It is usually boys that are afflicted with this behavior. Paula had beautiful green eyes and dark blonde hair. She was a pretty girl, but the students did not accept her very well. Paula's mother kept cats, lots of them. Paula smelled like a litter box. It was a very difficult thing to try to approach her about without sounding condemning of her or her home.

I left the topic alone for a while but the odor was really a problem. I talked with her teacher who had also noticed it. I guess I thought that the school nurse should handle this problem, so that it would not interfere with the instructional relationship that I had developed with Paula. After a period of time I decided to address the topic with Paula. I talked to her about the cats and said that I knew that she was aware of how the kitty boxes smelled, and that sometimes I could smell that on her. I told her with a smile that this was how I knew that they had cats at her house. As expected, she was very uncomfortable and defensive. I talked to her about how our hair picks up the odors around us, as does our clothing. I told her she could make sure that her clothing was not around the cats. We also talked about shampooing hair to get odors out. She was not happy about our conversation. She accused me of not liking her mother for having cats. We had to work on the problem for a few weeks. She eventually got over her defensiveness and even started smelling better. She apparently took some of the advice that I had given her. I was reluctant to meet her mother, as I supposed that she had heard about my concerns for Paula's odor. When I met her mother at a parent conference, the cat topic did not arise and we both got very comfortable with one another.

I had Paula, who stopped smelling, for second through fifth grade. One of her problems in learning was that she had much difficulty staying focused. Our classroom was right across the hall from the girls' bathroom. The hallway could be quite noisy at times. I worked with my class in developing skills for staying focused, as many of the L.D. students have this problem. Initially, when a class lined up in the hallway for use of the rest room, I would close our door to keep out the noise, and to keep the students' attention on their academics. Later as students got better at concentrating, I would leave the door open for more and more times when there was noise outside. I also did some exercises with the groups on staying focused. Paula had more difficulty than most and when we had gotten to the point where I was leaving the door open to the hall noise, she would ask if we could please close the door. I would tell Paula to try to ignore it and continue with her work. Paula's reading skills rose above grade level and her language skills, except for spelling, were exceptional.

I don't know if she were "staffed" out of the learning disabilities program in middle or high school. She returned to visit me from time to time. When she was near graduation from high school she came to see me. She was a beautiful well dressed young lady (with a pleasant smell!) and we discussed how she had done in high school. She had begun playing the cello in middle school and had become very proficient. In her junior year of high school, she had gone with some fellow classmates to Washington D.C. and played in a concert for the president. I was very pleased to hear this! She was on the principal's list for high academic achievement, and had her picture placed on the wall of the high school cafeteria, with the twenty seniors chosen for special recognition of their high school successes. Paula told me that her English teacher in eleventh grade found out that she had been in a L.D. program. The teacher said she just could not believe that, and asked what happened, how had Paula been able to achieve so much? Paula said, "I told her that Dr. Lancer taught me to concentrate." What a sweet endorsement!

Paula had an older sister who was married and had several children. The children both had some visual perceptual problems. This was a number of years after I had Paula as a student. Her mother, and her sister decided that Paula's sister should move into our school attendance zone so that I could teach Paula's niece and nephew. They moved into our zone and enrolled. They were both already identified and staffed into the special education program, and so they became my students. They were both exceptionally bright and very dedicated to overcoming their problems, as Paula had been.

The last news I had of Paula was that she was enrolled in college and doing well.

Entertain Me

Micah had a problem with fighting and cutting school. He lived with just his mother, who was a beautician, and an older sister who was in middle school. They lived in a small apartment off a very busy street, but very near to Micah's mother's place of employment. He was quite proud of his mother, but had a real chip on his shoulder toward school, teachers, and even other students.

He entered late in the school year when my fifth grade class was well under way. We had a routine that was working for that class. Micah came in on a Monday, the day that we always spent introducing the individual spelling lists and having a language session, that involved making sentences to illustrate the weekly spelling words. Micah came in dramatically and was sent back to get his spelling list. Before he started back he stared at me critically. "You're old!" he announced to me. Of course I was quite surprised. As this was later in my teaching career, my age was obvious. I was used to uncontrolled and petulant kids so I remained calm, looked at him quizzically and responded, "Oh? What gave you your first clue?" He was not ornery enough or quick enough to name his observations, but left in a huff to retrieve his list. On his return, he remained agitated and fussed with paper, pencils, and getting started. After a short period of time he remarked, "This is boring". I told him I was sorry he felt that way, but that was what we did on Mondays, and it "was as good as it gets". He continued to complain and finally, when I asked him what he liked to do, or would want to do, he just responded again with the boring aspect of the work. He then said, "you are supposed to entertain me." I told him that I did think that my job was to teach him—not to entertain him. He finished his work and left at the end of the session still in a foul mood. The other students had smiled about the age remark earlier and were even laughing when Micah said I was to entertain him.

Tuesday, Micah came in with the other fifth graders. He still looked unhappy to be there. I smiled at him, stood, stretched my arms out to each side, and burst into a rather quiet rendition of "Let Me Entertain You" (from the movie "Gypsy"). He was startled, but amused. The whole group laughed. Micah loosened up a little and we could all see a sense of humor that was not previously noticeable. He had a better time on Wednesday and as the week continued he was more and more cooperative. He fit into the group nicely, and was also somewhat of a class leader because of his humor and enthusiasm.

By the end of the year, Micah was very helpful and social. He brought lots of interesting topics and ideas to class and the group grew to love him. He was only pugnacious and getting into fights the first few weeks of his enrollment. At the end of the year Micah spent his last few days, before summer break, in my room assisting me with getting my classroom ready for the "check out" at the years end. The last few days of school the teachers are putting away things, doing a lot of review with the students, and the specialists (like myself) would cancel regular classes. Micah arranged with his teacher to come to my room to help me. He sorted all my colored construction paper by color and size, organized all my writing paper by space size, and put away our "free time" toys, puzzles, clay, paint, etc. I had never had such great help before. Micah turned out to be one of my very best friends.

Red Eye

Zantrell was much like Micah, a real fighter looking for trouble. Both of these boys were black in a school that was still predominately white. Zantrell came in the middle of the year. He had been diagnosed and placed in a learning disabilities program at another school district. He was in third grade and his mother came to talk to me before she brought him to our building. She reported that she had changed her apartment rental to one in our school district. She was worried about Zantrell, and she was at the end of her patience. He had been expelled from school several times and was told that if it happened again, Zantrell would be refused readmission to that school. He was a fighter and seemed to get into trouble almost every day. She was warning me and asking if we could help. Her past babysitter had refused to let Zantrell come to her house any longer, too many fights. She had moved, gotten a new day care center, and changed schools. Now she was warning Zantrell that he could NOT cause her anymore problems. His behavior had made it hard on her employment status as she was continually called to school to deal with him.

He came the next day, his head rather lowered and eyes not looking at me, nor the other students. He was in a group of three other boys in third grade. We all talked and Zantrell admitted having problems with fighting. We (the boys and I) questioned him about what caused the fights. Zantrell didn't seem to know why they started. He said, "The other kids just all want to fight me." He could not tell us anything that he thought might be causing the problem. He was a well built and rather tough looking boy. He thought that the kids just thought he looked fierce and they wanted to beat him up. The other boys said that he did look like he could hold his own in a fight. They gave him suggestions of how to "kid" his way out of a confrontation, or divert a mean approach. They offered to go with him on the playground at lunch and recess to help him get along.

Several days later, after one aborted fight assisted by his new friends, The boys were amused at what Zantrell was doing with his face. "Look!" they said, "Zantrell can look real scary". Zantrell gave me his scary look. He was pulling down the skin under his eyes. He rolled his eyes back up into his head so that we saw only red rims and the whites of his eyes. His face had an angry contorted look from his forehead and mouth. He looked ferocious. The boys gave him fearful looks and encouraged him to show them his "red eye" again.

I talked with Zantrell and he told me how he was so worried that he would be thrown out of school again, and that he did not want to fight. He stayed awake the night before. He thought and thought and finally decided that he needed to look so fierce that everyone would be afraid of him. He went into the bathroom to brush his teeth for bed and looked into the mirror, and practiced different ways to look very fierce. He finally came up with the "red eye". He was relieved, he thought he had finally found the answer.

The next few days the "red eye" worked well for Zantrell on the playground. I heard reports from other third graders about what a very mean kid this was who gave people scary looks. He did avert several fights. His buddies were amused, but Zantrell started looking at them with his "red eye" and they were upset. I talked with all of them and suggested that Zantrell try a "blue eye" or "green eye", that was friendly, to use with his friends. Or, I said, maybe just a friendly smile for them would be appropriate. They *all* agreed. Zantrell started smiling. He smiled sometimes to avoid a confrontation rather than using his fierce look. He began making more friends on the playground. I went out with him during his lunch times on several occasions. I talked with him and other boys around the basketball court. He learned how to ask others to join him in a game and he kept using his friendly expression.

Near Valentines Day, Zantrell announced to me that he thought he was in love. He was very interested in a pretty little Hispanic girl in his regular classroom. He asked if she could come in my classroom and play computer games with him on his Friday free time. I talked with his teacher and arranged the visit. Zantrell was beside himself. I had warned, "Don't use the 'red eye' on her. She will not want to be your friend". He agreed. They had a good time and Zantrell was *really* smiling. He made her a large red heart with a very sweet message that he composed. She was smiling. Zantrell was finding fewer occasions to use his "red eye" and by the end of the year he was mostly smiles. His "good eye" or nice expression was on his face most of the time. He had learned how to make friends and not instill angry responses on first acquaintance. Children are the best teachers for other children.

"Thank You!"

Allison was a very tiny kindergarten student. She had weighed only about one pound when she was prematurely born. The doctors worked hard to save the small life of this little girl. By sitting in numerous reviews of Allison's progress, I heard mom say, with some anger, "The doctors never told us that she could be severely handicapped". From the love and concern that I saw from her mother, I do not believe that this knowledge would have made any difference in the family's prayers for her survival. Allison was severely handicapped. She was still very small. She had muscular movement only on her left side only and it was limited. She could raise her arm a little above her waist and move it back and forth. Her fingers had little control, she could not speak, had very limited vision and was confined to a small wheelchair. But she had a beautiful smile and it was quick and powerful. The noises that Allison could make from her voice box were also limited. She had a high squeaky sound that all of us, that worked with her, began to interpret as "yes", and by her reactions and further noises, we were correct.

Allison's mother had read her legal rights. This was the nineties and the current national trend was to serve the handicapped child with special services *in* the regular classroom. Her mother insisted that the special education department give Allison the services for which she was qualified. These were; speech therapy, learning disabilities, physical therapy, visual therapy, and nursing services. She also insisted that these be administered (except for the diaper changing) right in the regular kindergarten room. This made it difficult for we specialists, for the classroom teacher, and made an added trip for the transportation department. Allison came on the handicapped bus with others in our building, but since she was only in kindergarten, she needed to be transported after one half day. I believe the children and Allison benefited from this placement. The class loved Allison and she loved school and her schoolmates. She also seemed more than appreciative to all the adults who attended her. I was assigned to her learning disabilities needs.

Allison was given a communication board by the handicapped services and ordered by her vision specialist. She did not like it and often refused to use it. The staff and parent decided that it seemed to irritate her eyes. Her mother had tutored her at home before she was old enough to enter school. She was very bright. She knew some of her letters and could spell her name. One had to place the letters in order and then ask her if it were correct. She would make her yes sound. I needed to schedule Allison in one block of time all by herself in order to go to her room and help her there. I really looked forward to working with her. She showed such delight when she learned something new. When we had a midyear conference with all the therapists, teacher, principal, and mother, it was determined that she knew all of her letters, the spelling of her own name and a few words to read. She could identify amounts from one to ten and also the numerals associated with the amounts. She was an excellent kindergartener. Her mother and I were the only ones who could testify to this academic knowledge as Allison's communication skills were so impaired. In working so closely and daily with her I knew what she had learned as did her mother. The classroom teacher had no way of assessing this. Her mother was greatly pleased with her progress, but all were dismayed that she would not try harder with the communication board.

I had decided that Allison could progress more if she could answer more than just a yes. If the answer were "no" we had to guess by her facial expressions and annoyed sounds that she made. She could squeal and cry out if she were really annoyed or distressed. I started taking her out of her classroom to the media center that was next to her room. We had privacy there, even though I was not working *in* her classroom as specified. Now we had no disruptions from the classmates. They did love to come by and hug her or see what we were doing. I worked hard with Allison and tried to help her to make a sound that was lower that would be different from her "yes". She put much effort into her attempts and tried so hard that she was frustrated. She did get a sound approximate to a "no" on a number of occasions. She seemed happy and I was very pleased. There was a problem. Apparently she worked so hard at making her sounds that she was too frustrated. Before, when she saw that I had entered her classroom, she was so happy, smiling, and making pleased noises. Now she was starting to fuss after I sat with her and started to work. Then one day when I entered her room, she even started to cry. I stopped working on the "no" for a while, thinking we could rest some.

There was a picnic for her classmates and a birthday celebration with balloons. When I came to Allison's classroom she was having a great time. They had all come in from the park next to the school building and were still in a state of excitement. Allison was very happy. She had a balloon fastened to her wheelchair near her left arm. Every little while she would bop it with her arm. I had a great idea. I started working with her on telling "amounts" I asked, "show me how old Allison is!" She bopped the balloon five times, and giggled. I decided to try some addition. I asked her, "How many are two balloons and then one more?" I showed her how to hit the balloon for a response. She giggled and then laughed louder. We spent the whole time doing some simple addition. She had a great time adding numbers one to ten. With the classroom teachers help we saved one of the party balloons to use for the next day.

While in a small variety store, I saw a small battery operated toy that said, "no" when you depressed the side. It was an almost defiant "no" but it seemed a great idea for Allison. She loved to manipulate my squeezey key chain that was supposed to be a frustration helper. I had given it to her to keep and I knew she would love the "no" toy. She did. We went to the media center and I asked her all kinds of silly questions just so she could answer no. I asked if she were ten years old, was it snowing (it was late spring) was I five years old, and other things to which she could immediately respond. I interspersed a few yes questions so that we would get the no more dramatically. She was thrilled and giggled every time she pushed the toy to say "no". Now, I thought, we must be able to get it from her voice as she will not always have the toy.

My next great surprise was with more of her verbal ability. I was asking her questions to which she could answer "yes" in her squeak. It was more of a sound like "eeeahhhnnKKK"

When I tried again for "no" and said make it lower, I got an "eeeewww" (as in blEW) I put these two sounds together for her, and then she made them. It came out "eeaank—eeeww". She seemed very pleased. I was surprised. I said, "Allison, did you say "thank you"? She squealed happily and said it again. I gave her a compliment that elicited a "thank you" she was delighted. I thanked her for a number of things so that I could use our new communication. She began saying thank you over and over. She thanked her teacher, the para who changed her diaper, and anyone that she could. She was so happy. I was even happier. On my way back to class I told the principal about my breakthrough and said I felt like Annie Sullivan (the teacher who taught the famous Helen Keller). Such a fantastic thrill and one of the best memories I have had of my teaching career.

After classes I phoned Allison's mother and told her I would like to stop by as Allison and I had something to show her. I drove to her house after school and encountered an excited mother and a giggling Allison. Mother had her out of her wheelchair and on the couch beside her. I sat across and made some compliments to Allison. She replied with her "thank you" and laughed so violently that both her mother and I were afraid she would fall off the couch. We all three laughed till tears came. Mom was really overcome.

The next day, and the days to come, Allison reveled in thanking everyone for everything. Shortly after this success, Allison's family moved out of my school attendance zone. I was very unhappy. I planned on using the bopping of a balloon or some other object for a "no" as it was completely different from her high squeal. I know Allison continued through school in the district, *in* the regular classrooms. I do not know what skills she has now.

Chapter Eight

WANTING A REAL FAMILY

I have saved this story for its own chapter. I wanted to tell it at the end of my memoirs of the learning disabled students. It is the hardest story to tell. It has been written over a longer period of time, is more complicated, and certainly more heart wrenching. And since I have stayed in touch with this student, the events are still changing.

Melissa's family had recently bought a new home, Mom, Dad and the two girls (ages seven and three) had a lovely new tri-level. The lawn was not yet in but they had spent Christmas in the new house, and the girls had loved their new bedroom. Dad's job was going well and he was able to better provide for his growing family.. Someone was coming to talk to him about a large debt and to make arrangements for pay. He was due at work (the family business) in just a few hours when he heard someone in the house.

His mother was the one who called 911. Her son had not reported to work and when it got quite late, and she had phoned several times with no response, she went to the new home. What she saw put her in a state of shock for years to come. His mother somehow managed to make that phone call. Melissa (the three year old) was the only one left alive and she was wandering about drenched in blood, her bloody face practically invisible, as she stepped slowly about dazed and whimpering. Bodies were all in different levels of the new house. Dad was on the main floor in a bloody heap in the family room near the garage entrance. Mom was in the lower bedroom, half off the bed, with stained bed clothes half covering her, and the older sister was in her upstairs bedroom on the twin bed, her blond head matted with blood. There was no evidence of a break in. The garage doors were open and the house unlocked. Mom and sister had been raped and all had been beaten with a blunt instrument (possibly a hammer). The case was later to be called the "hammer murders". Melissa was airlifted to emergency where she was put in intensive care—in an induced coma to give her brain time to lose its swelling, and her broken jaw—now wired shut—a little time to heal. Six weeks passed, touch and go, with no definite statement on whether little Melissa would survive. The public was much relieved when her condition was finally upgraded to poor. Contributions and benefits came from all over the country and everyone wished the little survivor well. Melissa was the darling of the police department and they bought for her the most incredible doll house that a child ever owned. It could fill an entire room and was exquisitely decorated and furnished. Small dolls were provided for hours of play—for a very sad and lonely little girl.

Melissa's paternal grandmother was to raise her and life continued to be difficult. Melissa's family had lived with grandmother and her sister had attended my elementary school just before they had moved to their new home. We had all heard, a couple of years later, that Melissa was coming to enroll in our school. The murder case was still quite celebrated and the perpetrator had never been caught. Each January the story would be retold on television and the public asked to report any information that they might have.

One day while at work in my school, I walked into the girls' restroom to quell the boisterousness of kids returning from the playground. I saw Melissa and without my glasses it looked as if she had an injured lip that was bleeding. "What did you do to your mouth?" was the unfortunate question that escaped me. "I was murdered", came the small child's reply. I tried to cover with the fact that her lip was quite red and sore from chapping and that she needed some vaseline or something from the nurse. I was much distressed at my comment as I was sure that "murdered" was more than true. Her earlier life, her ability to cope, her beauty, and what I later knew to be her potential, and even her family's love had all been killed. Melissa suffered from the symptoms of brain injury syndrome. She had learning disabilities from the trauma to her brain. She had much difficulty with short term memory and had difficulty concentrating. She was impulsive and (as is common in brain injuries) would often explode with vulgarities or swear words. Her favorite was, "ca-ca poo-poo" which greatly offended her very moral and inflexible teacher. Melissa was prone to temper tantrums when under frustration. She was made to sit at the back of the room away from the others, and would frequently dump everything from her desk to the floor in one of her fits of pique. One teacher reported that when she went in Melissa's classroom and the little girl had looked up and greeted her, the very incompetent teacher had very angrily said, "you keep still no one wants to hear from anyone like you!" Melissa still had many scars upon her face and no doubt took this as a physical insult as well as a behavioral one. After several reports of this kind, I spoke to the principal and insisted that the child be moved to another classroom. We had a new principal who was now able to understand the potential problems if the move were not made at semester time. Her new teacher was supportive and liked Melissa.

Later, after referrals for testing, the assessment completed, and a staffing held, Melissa was "staffed" into the learning disabilities program where I was to work with her for at least one hour daily. What a clever and wise little child she had become. It was easy to explain her own problems to her and have her gain insight. It took years to teach her to be patient with herself and when she did not remember what she had read or understand directions—to try again—several times if need be—until she could get it. Her reading, which had been below her grade level, improved immensely—she read better than her peers. Her comprehension came more slowly as she was still learning to deal with the memory problems. Meanwhile she told stories of misunderstandings and physical anger from her "mom", grandmother. Such insight to tell me that she felt her grandmother was angry at her because she, Melissa, had lived and the grandmothers' beloved son had not. She felt "mom" blamed her—and even hated her. She understood that grandmother would not talk about the murder with her because it was too hard. Another time she remarked that "mom" did not give hugs or kisses or say she loved her, as she was too hurt by her own tragedy to give affection to others.

Melissa had nice thick blonde hair and a lovely skin that seemed to be tanned year round. She had beautifully expressive green eyes with wonderfully shaped eyebrows—one with a slight scar through the middle. She adored a quiet and loving little black girl in the class that she attended with me. Erica had all the attention from her mother that any child would want. She was well loved, immaculately clean, wore the latest styled clothing, and her hair was beautifully coiffed every morning. Melissa came to school a little disheveled and did her own hair. Both girls had our special class at the very beginning of the day, and one morning we began a regular procedure of having me fix Melissa's hair. She asked that I do it like Erica's, which was numerous squares parted off, and small separate twists or braids all over, fastened by colorful tiny barrettes. The first morning we used my colored rubber bands and thereafter she and Erica brought me fasteners. In sectioning off the hair for her "do", I was astonished at the amount of injury that Melissa had endured. There were large scars throughout her scalp, but her wondrously thick hair hid all but a few of them right off the hairline, near her temple. In combing and fixing her hair I also noticed the fine ridge visible under her skin, that trailed down her neck below her collar bone, that was the shunt that carried the swelling from her brain. This shunt would stay with her for her lifetime. Hair fixing and other special attention was given each morning until we had a new ritual established. Melissa seemed to like school and her friends. She had good social skills and seemed to value and respect friendships.

For a language project in fourth grade she wrote an adorable but heart rendering little book titled "What Makes Me Happy". I still have her book which I intended to give her when she got older and had her own things. Each page lists something that could make her happy and has a clever and very artistic illustration to accompany the thought.

Some items of the list read: "A big bowl of macaroni and cheese, lots of Barbie dolls with tons of clothes for each, a twin sister like Martinique and Montinique (these were twin black girls in her grade level), gobs of make-up, and (last of all) a real mommy and daddy."

A few years later when Melissa became more difficult to control, "mom" would lose her temper and scream and hit at Melissa. Melissa saw her own provocations in this and said, "I make her angry when I ". When counseled that this was not good and she should try to control the relationship better, she replied that she did try but was unable. "Mom" was hitting and slapping her. As all young kids do in this society, she had knowledge of "child abuse" and was determined that her mom could not knock her around—nor could her paternal uncle, who never worked and drank beer all day and became angry at things that Melissa said. Again she understood this and said that mom was indulgent in this son because of the loss of the other son. One day, when she was particularly angry, she told me she was going to turn in her mom for child abuse. With the knowledge that she needed marks, bruises or the like in order to report the misdeeds, she backed off and said she would wait until she had some.

She came in on a Monday with her bruise. They had spent Saturday cleaning and Mom was stressed and had hit her with her purse when Melissa did not comply with some unreasonable directives. There were, in the small class with me, several other fifth graders who were in foster care and Erica, the girl who had been Melissa's friend for several years. "I am reporting her and am going to stay at my friend Erica's house for my foster home", she had said with a quiet resolve. I smiled at her, knowing how she envied that setting, "Melissa, it does not work like that. You do not get to choose your foster home. You are sent where the social services finds a place for you". I noticed how crestfallen she was to know that her plan for future happiness could not be fulfilled. The other two girls currently in foster care described some of the hellish situations where they had been. One told of much physical punishment, and the other of how she and her foster brothers and sister took money from a drunken caretaker to buy a delivery pizza when they were hungry and there was no food in the house. When the foster mother came out of the drunken stupor, she accused the children of robbing her and had them removed from her home. They carried the stigma of theft with them to their next placement. Melissa chose to keep still about her bruise and tough it out with her only real relatives.

Over the years I had counseled with Melissa's mother a number of times. She was in and out of therapy for herself and Melissa, through both her company's health plan and victim's assistance. We discussed how difficult Melissa's behavior could be and the reasons for it. She seemed understanding and supportive of Melissa, but at a total loss of how to handle her special problems. The numerous referrals for counseling during these several years were seriously pursued on several occasions, and Melissa's mom consistently devoted herself and Melissa to overcoming the problems and resolving the past trauma. Melissa remembered the attack and told about it on several occasions.

She received much attention from the schoolmates, but again showed her uncanny wisdom when she remarked to me, "Docky, I don't think they want to be my friend because they like me—for me—I think they want to be around me because of what happened to me—and because everyone knows me". A simple lesson in celebrity from one with such injury! Melissa was a very wise fifth grader with an understanding of friendship, a tolerance and understanding of the weaknesses of those who should be strong for her, and some patience developed for herself and her gradually improving academic problems.

Melissa moved the next year. She and her mom lived in a nice little apartment nearer the downtown area. She stayed in touch with Erica and they saw each other from time to time. Erica's mother was very nurturing to Melissa until the girls became very interested in boys. Erica's mother did not like the dishonesty and sneaking around that the young teenagers were doing. Melissa's mother became distressed with the disobedience and extreme interest that Melissa was showing in the opposite sex, it became more difficult for her to control Melissa.

Within a couple of years, I heard from Melissa's mother. She wanted to know if I could write a recommendation for Melissa's admission to a private boarding school, a high school in Arizona. I did and was happy to learn that she was accepted. Melissa spent the next three years in high school there. On summer vacations Melissa would come back here and visit her mother and her fraternal aunt. My daughter and I met her and took her to dinner on several occasions. Melissa still had a number of scars, although she had had numerous plastic surgeries over the years. She was having her teeth moved to allow an empty spot for a false tooth on the front, where the blows to her head had killed the root of her front permanent tooth. A wide scar was still running through one of her eyebrows and there was still some scarring over her bottom lip—the mark that I had first seen on her in the bathroom when she was in first grade. Melissa had bleached her hair and she wore it rather spiked (in a current fashion), and she she had become tall and willowy with a nice figure. Several young men turned to look at her when we entered the restaurants, as she walked with an air that commanded male attention. She seemed to have learned much over the years in high school. She conversed well on numerous topics and reported that she loved Shakespeare—and poetry. She was becoming a delightful young lady but still in need of much guidance. I was not sure how much she received from either her mom or the school counselors. She had been seeing a psychotherapist in the town near the high school, going for sessions on a regular basis. She seemed rather sophisticated about her therapy and talked some about her insights. I was to learn from her sometime later, that she had made a suicide attempt that had caused her to drop out of school, stay with her mom for a semester, and then go back to the school again. She seemed to have made a number of close friendships, all of which sounded like they were with somewhat dysfunctional students, that had banded together because of various adjustment problems. She reported some minor drug usage.

My next contact was by phone. She was living in town with some "roommates" that had difficulties. She had not graduated—had dropped out of school, would not follow her mother's directions, and was trying to get a job. She and her friends were of very marginal social adjustment. Melissa said she liked her friends and had plans to finish school and work. Her situation seemed somewhat like a "halfway" house or a shelter of some kind. No word again for a long time.

Melissa called from Tuscon. She was pregnant, without money, boyfriend long gone and a new one to take his place. The new one wanted to marry Melissa, give the baby his name and raise more family with her—only one small problem. He was drug addicted, the hard stuff, heroin, and Melissa loved David madly. She would call and tell me of her adoration of him from time to time. She was realistic enough to make the comment, "It's babies having babies". She said her own family had wanted her to have an abortion. She did not want one. She desperately wanted the baby to love, her own family, and David would be a part of that too. Phone calls would come with tears and fears about no food, no rent money, and David only wanting to get money for drugs. She was afraid that she could not do all that she needed to do to take care of a baby. At one time her plan included having the baby, being a stay-at-home mom for her baby, while babysitting for another lady in her apartment. The lady could continue her job, and Melissa could earn money while sitting. She said that David liked this plan. Each new plan included a job of some kind and Melissa finishing high school. David ended up in jail a few times. New roommates came and lived in Melissa's apartment, now being paid for by a maternal uncle who was trying to rescue her. Her uncle paid her rent and provided her with a car and phone. Her mother was sending a few hundred dollars a month—possibly from a fund that was set up for her when she first became The Victim. Melissa was angry at her mom, feeling that her mom had taken money that must have been for her education—from trust funds, etc. The uncle (maternal) was offering to assist Melissa in getting her money back. Her mother had not sent any for a long time but had begun sending it again.

David was "good at making money". He didn't get a job, nor did Melissa. One of her plans had been to waitress to make money. She said she was good at that and had done it before. David "hustled" which Melissa explained was to rip off the merchants and then go sell the loot. He could make maybe a hundred a day. He would pay for his drugs and some food. She now admitted that she had taken some drugs in the past, but was clean because of the pregnancy. Melissa was very pregnant, living off promises that David was going to marry her, and that they would eventually be very happy. David was in and out of jail and Melissa kept her faith.

The baby came, a beautiful healthy boy, blonde and blue eyed. He was given David's last name on his birth certificate. While David was not able to be at the birth (incarceration again) he seemed pleased with the baby and was determined to have the baby and Melissa for his family. I talked to David a few times on the phone and could attest to his sincere desire to do well with his life.

I didn't hear for a while and then Melissa called late one night. She had been alone all day with the baby. David was in jail again. There was no food in the apartment for the baby, and he was crying loudly. She had two roommates who were to provide food in exchange for living in the apartment that Melissa's uncle provided for her. The roommates had left at ten that morning and it was now ten at night and the baby had no food. She had given the infant water over and over again, whenever he cried. She laughed as she remarked that she could hear the water gurgle when she jostled him to stop the crying. I instructed her not to give him any more water, and to put him up over her shoulder, walk a slow rhythmic walk with him, and try to quiet him to sleep. She told stories of how he always cried, annoyed the neighbors and the roommates, and was responsible for complaints to the authorities. I was quite concerned that the frustration toward him, and her inability to quiet him could be a dangerous situation for an infant of only a few months of age. I asked Melissa to call me back in an hour or so to let me know if the roommates returned with the formula for the baby. She did. Roommates were so late returning as they had been picked up for shop lifting. They needed to steal something to get money to buy formula for the baby. Roommates were parents of two children who had been removed from their home by social services because of problems with drugs. They reportedly were very good with Melisa's baby.

Melissa called again off and on to tell me all that she planned to do, and to get my further encouragement. She had the baby taken from her the first of the year by the social services in Tuscon. Her reason, to me, was because she had left the baby with some irresponsible roommates (different ones) when she was taken into the hospital with a gall bladder attack. She had a number of things that she needed to do in order to reclaim her little boy, Darin. She had to report to a parenting class weekly, she had to report for a therapy session, she had to go to a drug abuse session, have drug testing (this because of David—she said), and she had to get a job. Along with these necessities she was also going to try to get her GED. There were numerous phone calls, sometimes hopeful, sometimes despairing. Occasionally she would be saying "Docky, I just don't think I can do it. It is SOOOO hard." Then the tears would come. She would acknowledge that she talked to her mother who had been very supportive and had told Melissa that "they" had tried to take Melissa away from her mom and her mom had proved them wrong. Something I had never known. She told me one of the social workers was questioning at a hearing if she knew right from wrong. She asked if I felt she did. Of course she did. I had known about her values since she was small. I told her I just felt that she had been influenced with drugs, bad company, terrible circumstances, and she had made some bad choices. "Oh," she said, "That's just what my mom said—she said I knew right from wrong—they are so hard on me and get me so confused. But my mom thinks I can prove them wrong. She says I can get Darin back".

Getting Darin back was her focus for the next six months. She had just that long before it would come up for a hearing again. She would call and report that the meetings were going OK. Then she started missing some. She was told no more roommates. David was in jail and she spent much emotional effort trying to decide if he loved her. When he got out he was clean for a while then began drugs again. Many calls came from her concerning how to get David back. He said he broke up with her because he was weak when he was with her. She needed to prove to him that she could be strong, for both of them, and doing all that she needed to do to get her baby back, would prove her strength to him. It was all about David.

Finally, she resolved within herself that, even trying to see him with interventions from his sister and his mother, he was not wanting to continue the relationship. She called from jail. She was in for shop lifting to get money for food—and for drugs. She finally admitted on her second call from a jail cell that she was into cocaine. Later she admitted to heroin and was relieved when she was "in" so that she would have to get clean. David did not seem to rescue her and was too busy kicking his own habit, off and on, and trying to raise bail. Only once did she ask me if I had money to send her. I never got into that kind of relationship with her, as she got the message that friendship and advice was all I was giving.

David was later replaced with several other short term friends who were in and out of her apartment and life. Then came Travis, he was another David. He was into drugs, irresponsible, but was going to make a life for her. He was on the run from jail down in Florida. The same calls came about drugs, jail, and no money. Now I was hearing that Darin was no longer an option. It was all over. She had lost him for good. She had said that an aunt had taken him to keep until she could earn him back. Now she said she had no idea where he was, they would not tell her. Months later I asked if she had signed over adoption papers for Darin. She said, "I don't know, I think so, I don't know what I signed—I was on drugs and so out of it—I don't know what I did. But I will never see him again. That part of my life is over."

The FBI came to her apartment and arrested Travis. She did knot know how they found him. She only said Travis had warrants against him. I explained it was more serious than that to take him back to Florida. Jail was where Travis remained for a long time. Melissa was calling and concerned that it would be so long before he could get out. She was off drugs again. Then on again. Travis was out of jail and was to be on parole. They would both be clean and life was again being planned. Travis's mother wanted them both to come to live with her in Florida. She had a lot of money and she would help them both. What a great opportunity.

A phone call several weeks later from Florida raised my fears for Melissa again. The house was nice, his mother was nice. Travis was not working and seemingly had no intention of doing so. They were not doing drugs. This was a stupid little town with no drugs available. Melissa was bored and restless, nothing to do all day but spend time with Travis's mother. Travis was out a lot with his friends. He had no time or interest in Melissa. One could tell that this was not going to last.

A few weeks ago (at this writing) a call came from San Francisco. Travis's mother threw them out. Actually, she threw Travis out and said that Melissa could stay there with her. I learned later that Melissa was pregnant again. Travis had been rude and defiant with his mother, and treated her with no respect. Melissa and Travis hopped a freight train and were living on the streets in San Francisco. There were three areas where the homeless could go. One was a cool trendy place for street people. One was for the horrible derelicts. And the one where Melissa and Travis had gone was in the gay area. The gays were good to the homeless and gave them food. There was tons of food in San Francisco. But they were cold, very cold. She had to wear three layers of jogging pants and sweaters to keep warm. They had brought all these clothes with them. Travis had no intention of working. He had run away and would be rearrested if he were found. He had jumped parole, was taking drugs part of the time, and just wanted to do "begging for food." He did not want to take care of or protect Melissa, as she felt he had promised. She could not get a job as she had no I.D. She sometimes did drugs—but did not really want to. She was calling from a pay phone with a very loud homeless person making strange sounds in the background. She said she would call back. She could not call her mother because her mother would say "I told you so", and so she didn't know what to do. I repeated numerous times that only she could make a change in her life, and that she needed to change the kind of associations that she was making. The noisy man was louder—Melissa would call back. She did a week later. She was in a laundromat and seeming to be a little more reasonable. She seemed more ready to rethink Travis. She said he told her she could go back to stay with his mother—he was not welcome.

I have not given up hope for Melissa. It is now almost Christmas again. Darin is long lost to the social services. Melissa is still on the streets in San Francisco. She and Travis are into drugs off and on—probably dependent on when they have the money. But I was much encouraged with her phone call at two A.M. last week. She cried off and on about how much she loved Travis and did not want to lose him. If she left and went to stay with his mother he would find someone else. When I agreed with that possibility, but also put forth an idea that it may not be such a bad idea—and that someone may be there for her that was not (as she called Travis) a "loser". There could be someone that could BE a good father for children, that she would want to have, and a responsible husband for her—would love her—and most of all would not have a drug habit to kick. She did respond with, "Why can't I have money, be comfortable, have a good life? I deserve it. His mother says he doesn't really love me or he would take care of me". I have said these same words to her, now they are coming from her mind and her heart. Maybe she can overcome being the victim. I sincerely wish this for her for this new year.

Dear reader, the last few paragraphs about Melissa were written almost ten years ago. Much has happened since then. I should not have been so optimistic about Melissa's ability to change the direction of her life. A close friend of mine, who is an expert on brain injury, informed me that if Melissa's injuries were in specific places in her brain, that she would be impaired in making long term planning goals and in pursuing them. I showed my friend where I had seen scars on Melissa's head. It was in very critical areas for ability to plan and to follow up on decisions. I wanted to let Melissa know that she needed to listen more to the advice of her mother and let her help Melissa with her plans. Melissa had been very open to my suggestions on dealing with her memory problems when she was a child. I had planned to discuss this the next time she called. I have not heard from her since I gained this information. But prior to my knowledge of her planning impairment, I heard from her several times which I did not record earlier.

After Melissa and Travis went to San Francisco, there were a number of calls about how Melissa feared that Travis only wanted to use her to help him to get more money while begging on the street. She reported that people were more generous when they saw her pregnant condition and she felt that possibly she was being used. Talking with her did not dissuade her need to continue their relationship. Melissa gave birth to a little girl, Kari. Because she had had an incarceration for drug abuse, Melissa was tested when she was in the hospital. She lost Kari to the social services. She and Travis had been back to his mother's home for a brief time. They left as both of them were concerned that Travis's mother had an interest in trying to get custody of the baby when it came. Back in San Francisco they lost the baby anyway. A relative of Melissa's was given custody and finally adoption rights to Kari. It seems social services try to place the babies with a relative of one of the parents. Travis was soon history. I do not know if it was Melissa's decision or if Travis just left. He was back in jail and Melissa had said that they both feared that Travis's mother was going to report him to the authorities for breaking parole. Melissa may have given up when he was arrested and placed back in prison.

Her saga continued. She returned to my area and her mother offered to buy her a condominium where she could live. Melissa was on social security. She had several very short lived jobs, was still associating with drug addicted persons, and was not very reliable. I suggested to her mother that if she were to buy the condominium that she buy it in her own name. Melissa was continuing to let these bad associates live in her apartment with her. It seems she would provide the housing and hope that they would contribute food. Sometimes it worked for a while, but I told her mother that it was dangerous to have her owning the condo, as the drug friends would influence her and she could lose it. I did not hear about what happened to that effort.

Later I heard that an old drug addicted friend of Melissa's was in town. Melissa was back into drugs. She was again pregnant. Her friend wanted Melissa to go back to California with him. She had told her mother that she would remain here. She wanted to get clean, have her child, and make a good life. She was making the effort and her mother was encouraged. She gave birth to another little girl named Echo. Her mother told me that she was much in love with the baby and things looked positive. When I heard again, Melissa had gone back to California with her boyfriend and the little girl was turned over to social services. Melissa's mother told me that she (the mother) had contemplated taking the baby but felt she was now too old to raise another child. The same relative that took Kari now had Echo. She had changed the baby's name to Vanessa.

Several years passed. The anniversary of the murder of Melissa's family came and the papers and television gave information about the unsolved, cold case. I called Melissa's mother and got very encouraging news. Melissa was back in town, alone this time. Her mother helped her get an apartment. She was attending a community college and had a desire to become a psychologist and counsel others to help them with their problems. At this time she was drug free, attending college, and making good plans for her future. She has seen her oldest child, now ten. The relative who has adopted her two girls does not want contact with her, nor have Melissa contact the girls. Melissa has seen neither of them since their infancy. I could not be too encouraged as Melissa is still in contact with drug addicted persons in her therapy settings. She is so easily drawn back into that lifestyle, and seems to be always pulled into a victim relationship. I can only pray that she will be able to maintain her focus this time. Life has been more than just difficult for this tragic young lady, who just recently turned thirty! However, she could still reach her goal of having "her own family".

Chapter Nine

OUR OWN KEYSTONE COPS?

I am at a loss to know where in this book to tell this tale. It is not about my students or even my area of assignment. This story does indicate the fallibility of educators, even those with long experience, making rather serious and sometimes crucial decisions that negatively affect young people for their lifetime. For some years after this occurrence that I will relate, I had former students that came back to visit and would say, "Remember when we had…" We would then ruminate about the time, and still be somewhat disturbed over it having happened at our school.

It was a rather cold morning in early spring, frost was still on the ground. Many children were in the habit of arriving early, even earlier than the school said it was alright for them to be there on the playground. This was because so many parents worked and they did not want to leave the children alone in the house after they left for their jobs. So, many would show up at school before the eight-thirty time given. The teachers came at eight, the cooks and custodian came one to two hours early to ready the school heating, unlock the doors (now we are locked all the time), prepare food, etc. Principals, at least the more responsible ones, often came earlier than the teaching staff. There was a fifth grade teacher who always came at least an hour early as he liked to do his preparation for instruction at school. He was a very dedicated and very effective teacher. He did not stay long after school as some teachers did, but was always there early. This cold morning both he and the custodian were in the teacher's classroom, which was a mobile out west on the playground. They looked out of the window and noticed a hump on the side of the south wing of the building, just off the playground. This was outside of the kindergarten through grade three classrooms. They were puzzled about what the large object could be and went to investigate. They were horrified to find a dead body. They, of course, called the police.

When I arrived at school in my appointed time, I found lots of confusion. There were several police cars and a number of staff members in the front of the building herding the students, who had arrived early, into the building. I asked one, "What is going on? Is there a problem?" My questions were met with hushed remarks about the fact that all of the students needed to go into the gymnasium and wait till further notice. They were NOT to go to the playground. or the mobile buildings. When I got inside, another staff member whispered that there was a body beside the building and we were preventing the kids from knowing that. There were no windows off the gymnasium and they would not see the police, nor the body beside the building. All staff members were to herd the students to the gymnasium or the cafeteria (it had no windows facing the south wing). There was, of course, crime tape all around the area near the body, but no one could see it from the areas where the children were allowed to go. None of the teachers in the south wing were able to use their classrooms. They had to meet their students in the prescribed alternative areas. The staff were all asked to man the entry ways and direct all the kids away from the dead body area.

I stood out on the front sidewalk to do my assignment just as an older black boy came running from the building. He had already been inside in the gym. His eyes were wide with fear and he was almost hysterical. "Wait", I called as I grabbed him by the arm, "Where are you going?" He responded anxiously, "I'm just getting out of here—there is a dead body out there!" I put my arm around him and tried to calm him. He was in tears and said, "I moved away from this kind of stuff. I moved here to stay with my grandmother to get away from this! They say there is no dead body out there, *but*, my friend and I saw it when we came early this morning. I just want to go home—to get away." I talked to him quietly and admitted that, yes, there was a body there, but the adults were trying to protect the kids from that information. They did not want them to be frightened. He wisely said, "They should not lie to us. We know better." I told him that the police were there, that he would be safe, and asked him if he would please not tell the other children what he knew, and try to help the younger ones stay calm. He agreed and walked with me back into the building.

As time for the start of school approached, we had most all of the students in places where they could not see outside. Some of the classrooms that had windows near the area had the window shutters closed so that no one could see out. The halls were clearing and the principal, counselor, and a social worker were conferring in the front hallway. Other staff members informed the rest of us that no one was to mention the dead body. We were just to say there was an investigation and that some of the students could not go to their own rooms. We were to keep it all quiet until the body was removed, which would probably occur shortly. Just as I turned to go to my classroom,which was in the opposite hallway, I ran into the young boy that I had stopped from fleeing the scene. He was headed toward the boys' restroom and crossed the hall to talk with me. He was quite confused, and now angry. "They are still telling us there is no dead body. I saw it. I know better. Why are they lying?" I again reassured him that the staff was just trying to protect the kids. I confirmed again that he was right. He had seen a body. I asked him again to just go along with the staff, act as if he knew nothing, and do not alarm the smaller children. He was not happy, but agreed. He said the lying was the biggest problem.

The school population had to wait until eleven thirty A.M.(beginning lunch time) to go to their correct classrooms. I had scoldingly remarked to the counselor and the social worker, who came into the hallway, that it was never right to lie about a situation, and that there were students who actually had seen the body. These two staff members had spent the morning going from class to class and denying all the rumors about a body. They were not happy with my comments and excused themselves by saying that, "This is what the principal asked us to do. That is what she wanted us to say." I really could not understand that excuse. They were the psychological experts. They should have stayed true to their knowledge and convinced the principal to handle the episode another way.

The reason that it took so long for the authorities to remove the body is that they assumed it was a murder as there was no weapon there. While examining, and finally moving the body, they found a gun underneath the body. It had been a suicide, and the dead young man had been on the roof, shot himself, fell to the ground, and covered up the weapon in his fall. It came to light that he had been a student in our school when he was a kid.

The group (principal, counselor, and social worker) decided that this would all be reported in the news, and that they needed to forewarn the students. All three spent the rest of the day going back through all the classes and admitting that, yes, there was a body. I never knew how they explained themselves to the kids. I do believe that the event of adults lying to them would have caused some distrust as an after effect. I know that I had much less respect for these three adults after this occurrence.

Chapter Ten

MY "SPECIAL" ADULTS

    I cannot complete these memoirs without mentioning special adults with whom I have dealt, along with all my special kids. There have been some very caring and exemplary people that I have had the pleasure of meeting in my teaching career. There have been a few teachers that I was sorry to see stay in the education field. Most teachers were at least average or good. These days there is much criticism naming "poor teachers" as the reason that education is faltering. I believe it is more the bureaucracy in the districts and the invasion of the state and federal government into the practices, and theories of teaching that have been at least foolish and often disastrous. In comparison, I have been exposed to numerous very poor administrators. Principals are very important to the character of their school. A very poor principal can negatively affect all of the programs in his/her building and make for a bad working environment, with depression and frustration engulfing the teachers who are trying to do their best. I have had about twelve different principals, of those I would grade one as superior, two as good, six as adequate, and three as very poor, even detrimental to the faculty and students. I have seen only three or four teachers that were bad enough to cause negative results for the children. Most were at least adequate, many I would rate as good and a good number, I felt, did an excellent job. As in all areas of employment, there are these same variations of performance. However, it did appear to me that in the area of performing as principals, there were substantially more poorly performing persons. We teachers used to use the old adage "those who can, do, those who can't, teach" and take it a step further. We would say, "and those who cannot teach become principals". This did seem to be very appropriate.

I would like to mention a number of extremely highly performing people in my world of education.

Anne

She was my mentor and supporter for my doctoral pursuits, and she was an excellent professor for adults in her program. Other colleges and universities were presenting mediocre programs in the educational field. Anne demanded superior performance and dedication from her students. She was careful in observing and advising students in fields that best suited their personalities and abilities. I took classes from several other universities over the years and was unimpressed with the programs or classes that were presented under her supervision. Other teachers that I have talked with had the same evaluation for the various higher education facilities. Everyone that I knew, that had taken courses from, or had professional connections to Anne, was extremely favorable in their comments about her. I saw her treat all of her professors, for whom she was the administrator, with extreme respect and support. She is highly intelligent, has given numerous speeches, published many professional articles, and was highly respected as a superior professor. She contributed very positively to the field of special education.

Kathy

She was one of the best school counselors with whom I was involved over the years. She really got involved in counseling and helping students. So many of the school counselors would give time and a superficial ear to the kids' problems, but they never seemed to really approach the individual problems. Most would do "artsy-crafty" projects, such as draw pictures, make dolls, or build exemplary bulletin boards, that made the counselor look good. It seemed that no one wanted to deal with the real problems and gain confidentiality with the individual students. One of the best compliments that I ever got from the children was when one of my students and her friend appeared at my door. It was after school and the halls were just beginning to clear. The two girls went to the room next to me and found that Kathy was not at school this day. She was only in our building three days a week. They stopped at my doorway and asked if they could see me. I said yes that I had time. My student gave me this unforgettable compliment. "You can talk to Docky. She is just like Mrs. G (Kathy). She will *really* listen to you and help you with your problems." The girl told me how distressed she was and talked to me about her fear of her stepfather who was going to be released from prison. He had served time for sexually assaulting her, and had his drug addicted friends misuse her also. I left Kathy a note explaining the problem, and giving her the girl's name so she could follow up with some counseling. Kathy took care of the situation immediately on her return to our school the next day. Many students came by to see Kathy after hours and before school. She had a very heavy caseload in our school as her reputation flourished. I heard many glorifying reports about Kathy over the years, from teachers and special educators throughout the district. I believe that Kathy is still helping the kids.

Gary

One of my very best helpers when I had my own classroom in my last school, was the custodian. Gary should have been a school counselor. He had started to take some college classes but had to quit for lack of money. When he first came to our building, the student population was very excited. There was a rumor that he had been a football player for an important team in the NFL. He had been a football player in high school and was acting as a referee for high school games for extra money. He was large and muscular and really could have been playing still. Gary connected well with the kids. The school was going through a big change in the make up of the population. We were changing from an almost all white school to a large number of Afro-Americans in our enrollment.

Gary was black and he understood my students who were also black and struggling with learning problems. He was a great role model. I had scheduled a group of my older students, a number of which were black, for the last period of the day. Gary usually had most of his work completed, and had a little time before his many chores at the school dismissal. He would come into my reading group and read along with the boys in my group. They loved it. Teachers and staff were not used to the new racial influence in the building. The boys in my group would sometimes complain that the paras, teachers, or others in the building were racist. I would ask Gary to come and help with our discussion groups to solve such problems. He could always help the boys to see if they were being righteously accused because of their poor behavior, or if there were an unjust punishment or attack. The guys trusted Gary and he helped them to sort out the truth in what was happening. Sometimes they were correct in their accusations and Gary and I would help them with ways to react to the situations.

Gary was also a good friend. The male teacher across the hall and I both had bought evaporative coolers to help with the early fall and late spring heat in our building. This school has recently been remodeled and now has air conditioning, but about fifteen years ago it was very uncomfortable. My windows were on the east side of the building and got the early morning sun. I had no blinds to cover the windows. Blinds had been removed when the classroom had been divided into two rooms several years earlier. The male teacher across the hall had blinds, but his windows were on the west side and right above the "black top" on the playground. The heat from the asphalt made his room unbearable in the afternoon. Gary reported to work at least an hour before the teachers were assigned to come. He would come into my room and the other teacher's room and turn on our coolers to make it more comfortable when we arrived. I was extremely grateful when he started getting ice from the kitchen and putting it in the coolers to make it even better. I was so sorry when Gary took an assignment at the administration complex and was no longer at our school. A large number of students were also saddened. He was very good for the kids.

Rosie

One of the principals that I mentioned as being very good, was Rosie. She seemed to understand kids very well. She was single, had never been married or had any children of her own, but she had great "people skills". Not only did she understand kids but she really understood her teachers. She knew all their strengths and their weaknesses. She was clever enough in her supervision that she tried to help teachers develop better skills, and she was quick to recognize their strengths. She was very helpful to me as we often talked about my troubled kids and their needs. We would also discuss next year placements for my group. She was interested in seeing that kids had a teacher that could help them with their specific problems. She also knew most of the children in the school and tried to match kids with appropriate teachers, considering the personalities of both. I had only had two other principals who seemed interested in assisting me with any kid related problems or even listening to them. I was always confident that my students would receive appropriate discipline at her hands. She is the one who assisted much with our satanic case involving Neva.

When Rosie retired, the entire school population, kids, teachers, office and kitchen staff, and even the paras were sad to see her go. The music teacher helped the fifth graders write a song for her. We had a special program, with large posters containing good wishes that covered the walls in the gymnasium where we held our assemblies. Everyone was teary eyed except for Rosie. I still don't know how she held it all together, with the many sensitive comments of appreciation from adults and kids alike. A few days later, we had a lovely retirement dinner for her at a local restaurant and she still seemed cool and in control at all times. When others have retired they have occasionally returned to visit. Rosie never did. She did come once, after school a number of years later. A former principal of our school was having her ninetieth birthday celebration, and some of the former teachers had a special tea for her in our newly renovated media center. Rosie looked around and admired the improvements in her old school. She had a number of hobbies, one of which was genealogy, which now keeps her active and interested. She made a very easy transition from work to retirement.

Dr. HUGE

He was extremely tall, about six feet, five or six inches. So the fifth grade boys called Dr. H. Mr Huge or Dr. Huge. He had played basketball throughout his college years and still loved to shoot hoops. I had Boston fern plants hanging from my ceiling tiles, that he needed to duck from or hit his head. The boys were amused by that. He was undoubtedly the best psychologist that I had worked with in the school system. The troubled boys that he worked with in our school were privileged to get to go with Dr. Huge and shoot hoops in the gym. He was great at counseling and really connected with the kids. He had a very keen insight into finding hidden causes and fears in his clients. He did all the intellectual and psychological testing needed in our school and was also assigned to two other schools. He had no office. His room assignment, for when he was in our building, was in a small room to be shared with the speech therapist and two other part time staff members. The room had its fill of adult desks, and almost no working space. The other "roommates" let Dr. Huge know that there was no room for him. At the time I was sharing my room with another L.D. teacher who was only there in the mornings as she served another school in the afternoon. Dr. Huge did most of his counseling work while walking with the kids and talking, or informally tossing basketballs in the gym. When he needed space for testing, he often used the gym teachers office/storage room where there was a desk and several chairs. The school did not have a computer for him to use when in our building, so I shared mine with him. We both did files and information for the special education department, and needed to compile test scores and write up results on the forms that were on the computers. I also invited Dr. Huge to share the room as necessary. He was able to use the other L.D. teacher's desk and instruction area when she was not there in the afternoons.

Dr. Huge was very perceptive and could see hidden problems in the children that teachers and other therapists had missed. He would find additional tests that were above and beyond the regular testing protocol used by the district. In two of his other schools, he was instrumental in detecting several severely disturbed students, with possible dangerous tendencies. He had a number of projective tests for diagnosis, and his own keen insights, that made him exceptional in determining specific problems in children. This was true also for his work with adults. He later did much work with several different counseling facilities, then worked for several years as a "profile specialist" for the police force in a large nearby city. I was so pleased to work with him as he was one of the few psychologists, with whom I had teamed, who would further investigate some of my observations and concerns about specific children that we were testing. He also helped me to get a "double identification" for some of the students in my case load. These kids were learning disabled but were also very bright. Dr. H. would assist me in gaining permission to have them tested for the "gifted and talented" program in our district. It was required that they have a very high I.Q. score. Dr. H. knew which I.Q. test would best access the skills that we both saw in the child. They would then be labeled both "learning disabled" and "gifted and talented". I was amazed at his predictions of later problems that some children would exhibit. He was able to see much beyond the obvious and really understood dysfunctional personalities. One student in our school who had excessively bad behavior (mostly outside of school and in the home and community) but managed to remain in regular classroom, was keenly observed by Dr. H. He predicted a bleak future and possible criminal activity for this boy. He was right. The boy ended up controlled by drug addiction, breaking laws, and finally he broke into a neighbor's home looking for drug money. He killed the older woman living there alone. The young man is still serving time.

Dr. H. loved to play chess. He had an unusual way of teaching chess moves, using hand signals to indicate the manner in which individual chessmen could be moved. My students were able to understand the intricacies of plays after working with Dr. H.'s tutoring. I did not play chess and only could help the kids with which pieces were allowed to make which moves. Dr. H. and I started a chess competition for any of the kids in the school that were interested. It was after school one day a week. We had a large number of students who came and so we started a "chess club". Dr. H. taught the kids how to win in just five moves! They were very impressed. I was only helpful in keeping charts on the winners and assisting in calling moves as legal or not. We had the chess club for several years, until Dr. H. was assigned to different schools. He was very good at de-escalating students that were out of control, and so was moved to some higher risk schools to help manage discipline, where help was more sorely needed. I continued the chess club with a fifth grade teacher who wanted to be involved. We used her classroom as it was twice as large as mine. She wanted to include more students, so we enlarged the club to include board games of all kinds. The principal gave the other teacher some funds to assist in purchasing the needed games. Dr. H. is no longer with the school district. He is still assisting the police department, and has a counseling practice with several other colleagues.

Linda S.

In the late '80s, because of the many state and mandated programs for the handicapped, the district was still increasing its capabilities of servicing all handicapping conditions. I believe that most of the severely handicapped children had been receiving assistance in their home school if possible. Many of them were receiving home bound services from school specialists and remained at home. With the new laws for the "handicapped" the school districts were required to provide more and more services. So our district determined that there should be several classrooms at the elementary level to provide for the severely handicapped. Our school had a lower enrollment as the community changes (by age of the housing developments and the population aging) were proving to produce less school age children. We were in the older section of the city and now had some empty classrooms. The needed renovations to our building consisted of: remodeling bathrooms in two classrooms for handicapped accessibility, remodeling of the hall bathrooms for the same purpose, Placing braille plaques at each door, and hand rails attached to the walls throughout the school. It seemed as if they began the "railing", went up and down all halls, on out the doors, (and I fantasized) went on down the street with the railings, and on out to the main highway. We had railings everywhere. There were two classrooms for the children, another classroom was set aside to house the specialists who would provide services. In the specialists' room there were desks for a speech therapist, a learning disabilities teacher, a vision specialist, a nurse para, and a physical therapist. The center of the room was also equipped with mats and other tools for the physical therapist. At one side of the room there was an area with tables for diapering the incontinent students. There were two classroom teachers that were recently trained for "special education", but had little expertise in working with severe handicapping conditions. A number of the students were confined to wheelchairs, some did not speak much, several were blind, and a majority were mentally handicapped. It was impossible to do group instruction, there were too many in the room to get much individual instruction accomplished. As a result it seemed to be poorly conceived and staffed for real education of the children, and the teachers were ill trained. One teacher became known for using the television in excess. Everyone knew that she was often watching the soap operas.

Linda S. was the speech therapist assigned to the special program. She was brilliant, well trained but, unfortunately for her, outspoken. She was from New York and had the regional accent plus the New Yorkers attitude of being less sensitive about giving or receiving criticisms. Linda was aware of the inabilities of the others on the staff. Being a pilot project, there were many mistakes made. Linda was not shy in trying to correct things that seemed so very wrong. She was excellent in her field and I believe it bothered her to be around such incompetence. From my observations, I noticed correct procedures from the physical therapist, vision therapist, and Linda. Everything else seemed rather haphazard and poorly managed. The staff for the program worked out the time scheduling, which was one of the programs' few strengths, allowing Linda to at least do her part correctly. The classroom academic instruction was poor and even negligible. The program did provide relief for the parents, some good socialization for the students, and a single place for the legitimate therapists to provide services. The program was given a grant for the following year. All the educational staff were rehired, except for Linda. She seemed to be the only one critical of some of the policies and procedures that could have been much improved. The program continued on in our building for about five years. Improving yearly with better classroom instruction and practices.

Linda, not rehired, took a year off and went to the university. She remarkably earned a doctorate degree in one year! In addition, she had her second child that same year. Linda is now a noted expert on brain injuries, speech therapy, and mental impairments. She works independently and with the state to provide services for home bound and severe cases. She has been an inspiration to me and to all of her colleagues.

Mr. C

My first principal, in the second district in which I taught, was the most remarkable administrator that I have ever met. He loved kids. Kids loved him. That is remarkable for a principal. His discipline was amazing. He would walk into the noisy, crowded cafeteria and it would become quiet. This was not out of fear, but out of respect. When he approached the front of an auditorium to announce an assembly, the talking would stop and all attention would be correctly directed to the front of the room. This great respect was noticeable even when he just entered a single classroom. The students all stopped what they were doing, stopped any conversation, and addressed their attention to him.

Mr. C. was a tall man and quite slender. He did not have the physical appearance that would cause this kind of respect. It was that all the children, who had any dealings with him for disciplinary reasons, knew him to be strict but fair, and considerate but honest. I never heard any criticisms of him from any of the teachers with whom I worked.

Lucky for me, Mr. C. had a great sense of humor. It was near Christmas and this was back in the days when schools recognized that it *was* Christmas and not just "winter holiday". For an art project, my third graders had made construction paper cut outs that went all across the front bulletin board above the chalkboard. This narrow but long bulletin board was beautifully decorated with "the twelve days of Christmas". There were all of the items, from the partridge in the tree to the lords, ladies, drummers, etc. My students and I were proud of the depiction. My teacher friends came to see it and the kids asked if they could sing the song. We asked the guests if they would like to hear it, and they felt obliged to say yes, they would *love* to hear it, and so we began singing the song for our visitors. Mr. C. mentioned in the teachers' lounge one day, that he had heard we had a great bulletin board. I smiled and invited him to come and see. He responded that he would decline. He was sure the artwork was great, but that he absolutely hated that particular song. It was one of his least favorites. Maybe he would come when the kids were not there. He said he suspected that I would not sing the song on my own. A few days later he came to our classroom with a rather important message for me. He smiled and acknowledged the famous bulletin board. I turned, smiling to my class, and said, "Would you like to sing the song for Mr. C." They were soooo excited. The song is very long. I know it was even longer for Mr. C. He was brave and stood there till the very end, then smilingly thanked *all* of us. He thanked me again later, personally.

I will always be grateful to Mr. C. for giving me David as a student. If it had not been for this, I would undoubtedly have continued working in regular education. I have really felt such personal growth and understanding by my involvement with children with special needs. It is so impressive to see what children and adults, can do when they have limitations that they need to overcome.

Mr C. moved from our state. I heard he was again assigned a principal-ship in his new location. That district was very lucky to have such a great educator. The principal who followed him, in the school where I was teaching, was another story. He loved discipline and had a large wooden paddle hanging on the wall to help him assert his authority, he did use it often. Mr. C. only had conversations with offenders, and his approach gained much better cooperation. These days a principal would probably be fired for even having the paddle on the wall.

Jeff

Whenever I hear the expression "a prince of a man" I think of Jeff. He was remarkable in his ability to pull the best from others, whether students or co-workers. Jeff always dressed well and professionally. He was manly in appearance and attitude. His students greatly respected him. He had fifth grade and in the spring the fourth grade students would start talking about how they hoped to be in his class the next year, especially the girls, as he was also quite handsome. When there were guests in the school, or even substitute teachers, Jeff went out of his way to make them feel more than welcome. He had a way of communicating to his fellow employees that made them feel special. He would direct group conversations to members who were not being included. When you talked with him one-on-one, Jeff always wanted to know about you, your interests, your problems. Jeff had a wonderful family, a beautiful and gracious wife and two gorgeous girls. One of his girls has grown, finished college and is now a teacher herself. The other daughter is now in college. Both girls excelled in sports and have earned scholarships.

Jeff's teaching was very much "Jeff". He always arrived more than the regular forty-five minutes before class as the job demanded. Jeff was always there about two hours early. He had impeccable lesson plans, handled his grading and reports in more than an adequate manner. Jeff had a special place on his chalkboard where he placed a daily time-line each day. The students all knew what to expect, and when. His class was very orderly, but not overly controlled. He had great discussions and was always open to listening to his students. His teaching was exemplary. His students could expect several reports assigned per year. They were expected to do some research, organization and composing. He was training them for abilities needed in the upper grades. In addition to making the written report, Jeff expected his students to present their work orally to the class. He would make a schedule for the reports so that the student knew when he/she was to perform. He built great skills for his students. Jeff was well organized and did excellent planning. I was often in his class and did get to hear his lesson presentations on occasion. There were a couple of years when our district had a shortage of substitute teachers. We specialists who did not have a full classroom, were on a schedule to cover for regular classroom teachers, if absences required it. I did on one or two occasions have the privilege of covering Jeff's classroom. His class would have been my choice because of the organization and the behavior of his students.

Literature was a favorite subject for Jeff. Right after the period, he would read daily to his class from great writings. He read with expression and instilled the habit of reading into his students in his classes. His dramatic voice was heard outside in the hallway each early afternoon. I always smiled and envied the students hearing his reading. In the earlier days of my teaching career, Jeff would have been a principal's dream, he did everything so well. These last few years administrative changes brought about the idea that all teachers should present every lesson in the same manner. This was not a good omen for Jeff. He was himself and did things a perfect "Jeff way". Teachers were even being told that they did not have a place in their time schedule for the "reading aloud". This had been one of Jeff's and his students' favorite times. The education system was changing, and not for the better. Most of the classroom time needed to be given for preparation for the state assessment tests. These were being used to judge teachers and also the principals. Lots of the niceties and personal things that teachers had done in the past were taken from them. No more literature enhancement! In addition the district had begun using "coaches" to help the teachers to improve.

These coaches turned out to be selected by the principals and were often just personality favorites of the school principal. They had no training and were often much less qualified than the teachers whom they were coaching. In one case in our building, the school counselor, who had never taught in a classroom, was designated as a coach. My last year in the district I was present in the teachers' lounge on the occasions when three different teachers were in tears over the the conferences that they had with their coaches. The manner in which Jeff taught was not one that could be easily emulated. Not many people would have the skills. Jeff surely did not want to change his methods of instruction to appear just like the teacher down the hall—and throughout the entire district. He was his own person. He had no option now but to take an early retirement to escape the nonsense. He is now substituting in the district, but is very mindful of which schools and grade levels that he agrees to teach. I fear for how all the schools will so change.

Dick

Another fifth grade teacher, who was a close friend to Jeff, was the master teacher Dick. He was a great influence on Jeff and was one whom Jeff looked upon for advice and mentoring. Dick had been in the district for many years. He had once lived across the street from the school where he was teaching. He was a staunch supporter of the parent teacher group and he was the teacher who would always volunteer to handle the student color guard, the group assigned to take care of daily raising and lowering the flag. I think there are now no more "color guards". Usually the custodian unceremoniously does this job. (Gone are the cub scouts, pledge of allegiance, raising of the flag, etc.) Dick was much like his successor in grade five, in that he taught citizenship, responsibility, and morality, not just in speech but in his actions. Dick thought his students should learn to be responsible in knowing about money, budgeting, and how the monetary system works. This information was not in the curriculum, but Dick taught it in his class. He had his classes look at the daily newspaper and see how the stock market worked. He had them select stocks and pretend to invest, then check their progress. He also made use of the daily paper to address the news items and current events. Jeff also used the newspaper. Dick was there before such strong use of the internet. He is now retired but if he were here he would be teaching his students how to appropriately use the internet. He continually talked with his classroom students about responsibility in life. He was often kidded about his lectures by his students who returned to visit. Many of them returned to see their old fifth grade teacher and let him know how much he had influenced them in their lives. Dick once had a student who returned, when he was a mayoral candidate, to let Dick know how much he had helped him, not just when he was his teacher, but the man had great memories of life lessons Dick had given. These things have no place in today's classroom agenda.

Dick was very concerned about each child. He took the parent teacher conferences very seriously. He loved to counsel with the parents, and liked to also have the student in the conference. Dick had three boys of his own and gave great guidance to them as they grew up. He was a model teacher and a model husband and parent. The other teachers admired Dick and often asked him for advice, both in teaching and in more personal skills. He was usually chosen to be the "acting principal" when the principal was out of the building. Everyone, especially the children, respected his sense of fairness and great disciplinary skills.

He instigated the "breakfast group" that we had for a number of years. On Fridays about eight or so of us teachers would meet at a breakfast/lunch restaurant about two miles from the school. We would come early in the morning to be finished in time to get to our building at our assigned time. We had wonderful conversations and built great friendships over the years. Dick was very much the leader of the group. At the end of the school year, when we had our rooms all packed up and cleaned, and our paperwork ready to be checked out, Dick promoted a group sing along in the music room. The music teacher would play the piano and we would sing the "oldies". Then we started doing this at Christmas and spring breaks. We had a great comradeship that developed. I see none of that in the schools today.

There is a news program that celebrates citizens who contribute much to their community. I sent in Dick's name and resume, but he did not win. He was not devoted to just one charitable situation as those who have received the award. Dick had a number of things and places to which he gave time and assistance. He had moved out of the city into a small nearby town which demanded his commuting. He was a volunteer fireman for his town and gave many hours of service there. He was also very active in his church with many fine projects that he helped organize and run. In addition he was active in the town's activities for Thanksgiving turkey shoots, feeding the poor, and other causes. His wife and sons were also admirable citizens and remain so to this day. Dick retired about fifteen years ago, he is still remembered by the teachers that taught with him and are still employed. He and his wife moved to another state, where they continue to assist in lots of community causes and stay active in their church. They enjoy gardening, and grandchildren. Dick, like Jeff, is also a great example of a remarkable educator.

Linda P

No physical therapist ever went the extra mile to the extent that Linda did. She was a very efficient and professional person who was always exceptional in her testing and reports at staffing conferences. I dealt with her many times when we were assessing students' needs. She went way beyond what was expected of her. Linda was a pretty and cheerful teacher. She always had a smile and was extremely connected to those children that she served. Linda had a physical strength that benefited her in helping her clients to move. She was extremely dedicated and one could tell that she had great love for her work and for her students.

Allison, the severely handicapped kindergartner that I wrote about earlier, was one of her students. Allison would always smile and make happy noises when Linda arrived for their sessions. Allison's sense of humor and Linda's personality worked very well together. I have never seen a teacher of the handicapped with a greater compassion for others than Linda.

I had a third grade student whom I was seeing for reading difficulties. She had very poor posture and walked with a slight slump. She was tiny for her age and her small frame seemed too frail to hold her body upright. I was concerned that she may have had spinal scoliosis. When Linda came for an appointment with another student in our building, I stopped her and told her of my concerns. She found time to come and do an informal evaluation of the young girl. There was no spinal curvature that Linda could notice, but Linda was also concerned about the posture and movement of this child. The girl had been diagnosed and placed in my program only. If Linda had seen a severe problem we would have had to have a referral and further assessments for the student. Linda spent a lot of time talking with the child's parents, giving them information on some exercises and other things they could do to help their daughter improve her posture. She gave me a list of things I could have the girl do when she came to my class. There were a few easy exercises, sitting movements, and walking movements. The student and I made a game of about ten minutes daily when she did special movements, or exercises, before we worked on her reading. She was a little embarrassed around her four other classmates so we included them in some of the postures and moves. They all enjoyed it and the moves were things that would also help their postures. Linda continued to check periodically on the little girl the rest of that year, and followed up on her progress the following year. She did show great concern and help for someone not even on her "case load". Linda still works for the district. They are extremely lucky to have such a dedicated teacher

Liz

The first grade teacher that offered to take Melissa, when her classroom teacher was so inappropriate with her, was fantastic. I never saw her presentations but I saw her results. She always had students that learned to read easily. I was amazed when she told me that she never understood phonics. Her students all were great readers by the end of the year. I did know that she used the old readers that had the phonics in them, but to hear her say that she did not understand phonics was a real surprise. She certainly did understand the children. She was the favorite teacher for all of her students when they arrived at the end of the elementary school experience. Students who were not in Liz's class were also fond of her. She had lots of visitors from other classrooms before and after school. These kids came with their friends that were in Liz's room, just to see Liz. I did observe her with her students in class but had not observed any "lessons". What I saw was a very friendly and accepting teacher who really connected with her students.

Liz was physically beautiful and looked much like a current very popular movie star. Liz had many health problems. She had about three years where she was absent for a space of time because of surgeries. She had been born with a hip displasia and was confined to a wheelchair until the end of her high school years. Liz was making up for lost time. She had a plethora of male friends all wanting her attention. She more than made up for not being able to date earlier in life. She had a hip replacement surgery and was now jogging, dating, and having a wonderful life. She was having difficulty with her digestive tract as she had scar tissue that developed. She did have to have surgery about once a year for the build up of her scar tissue. During her hospital stays her room was occupied with many visitors, mostly male admirers. She had lots of flowers and gifts along with her visitors. Some of the parents whose children were placed in Liz's room were concerned after the first several operations. They did not want their child to have a teacher who was absent for a prolonged period, but the reputation of her teaching skills, and the children's desire to be in her class outweighed their initial concerns.

Because of her hip surgery, and her related problems with scar tissue, Liz was told by her doctors that she should not try to bear children. Liz was one to do what she really desired to do. She finally selected one of her many suitors, got married and promptly had a beautiful little girl. She managed the child birth with some difficulty but was glad that she had done it. She continued to teach and in two years she gave birth to her second daughter. Her doctors were upset with her and convinced her to have surgery to prevent further pregnancies. Liz had not gotten over how nice all the attention from so many men had been. She had difficulty in her marriage because of this. Her husband was an actor and decided that he needed to go to Hollywood to further his career. He was making all the preparations to follow this career and was still living with Liz, while she was being more than attentive to other boyfriends.

One morning Liz awoke with a start. There was a bad smell in her house. Her head was dizzy. She awoke her two daughters who were sleeping soundly, and called 911. There was carbon dioxide in the house. Liz and her two daughters were taken to the hospital. Her husband was found dead in the attached garage. He had taken an overdose of tranquilizers, turned on the car engine, rolled up the windows, and thus committed suicide. Liz and her daughters were treated at the hospital for their lungs being filled with the poison. The little girls were there several days, Liz only one. The poor family of her husband, Liz, and the children were devastated. There was a lovely funeral planned. Liz and her husband had no insurance. They were in the process of divorce. Many of Liz's close friends and a number of her fellow teachers contributed money to assist her.

Liz became less of a "play girl" and was very dedicated to her girls after this. She continued to be an exceptional teacher and has transferred to different schools over the years. She has always been in first grade. She loves the younger children. Her own daughters are grown now. I recently read in the school district new releases, that Liz had been awarded a tribute given to "the best teacher". I'm sure that she deserved it.

Sarah

Sarah and her family and her extended family, her husband's parents, lived right across the street from the school. Her children all attended the school from kindergarten to grade five. Sarah and her husband were always very active in the parent teacher organization. They both had served as president from time to time. They performed many volunteering jobs for the parent organization and for the school. They would help with back to school programs, book fairs, family nights, etc. You could always count on this family to make the occasion successful. Sarah worked for the city and had a highly responsible job. The more she was involved with the school, the more she wanted to actually be a teacher. She got enough hours of credit at the local college to get her teaching certificate. She did her student teaching at her children's school. She had an excellent supervising teacher under which to do her student teaching. He was one of the very best in the district. He did lots of extra projects with his students. He gave extra classes to his fourth graders to help them with using computers. He trained them with using the internet long before the district began hiring a media specialist to do this job. He also worked with the "gifted and talented" program to help the advanced students to do research projects on the internet. Another project that he sponsored was the after school chess club. He was an excellent teacher to help Sarah complete her student teaching, as she also did many extra things to enhance her class programs.

When she finished her training, Sarah began teaching in the same school. The principal, teachers, and students were all delighted to have her on the staff as a full time, regular fifth grade teacher. She did many remarkable projects with her students over the years. It was so great to see a parent who was so very interested become an active member of the faculty. When her sponsoring teacher left for another district assignment, Sarah took over the chess club program. She also had many advanced instructional programs relating to computer usage. Her knowledge of research helped her in having excellent instruction for her students in report writing and preparation for the middle school curriculum.

Sarah's three children all completed their elementary education at our school. They were all exemplary students with very high achievement. Two of them earned full scholarships upon completing their high school education. All three were in the gifted and talented programs in elementary school and had many honors throughout their middle and high school years. All three are now pursuing college degrees. Sarah continues to teach in the same school and all in the community recognize and honor her service and abilities. She is truly a master teacher Judy

One of the very best school cooks that ever I had run into was Judy. She was from Japan and had married an American soldier who was stationed in her country. In Japan, Judy was very well educated. She was a higher education teacher in dressmaking, nutrition, and cooking. When she came to our country and our state, she was not qualified as a teacher. We require student teaching and a state history class for certification. She did not have the correct coursework for teaching, so she was hired as the chief cook for our building. The food was as tasty and outstanding as a school lunch room environment could provide. While school lunches were being prepared, Judy found time to make special dishes in her back office, area using small electrical appliances and her own ingredients. She would treat the teachers with special dishes from her culture. Teachers began bringing Judy unusual ingredients that she could use for her special dishes. Judy's direct supervisor was aware of the extra cooking, and she also imbibed when she could be in the building. The principal knew of Judy's dishes and said nothing. I would rather imagine that the district superintendent would have been a little upset as this was not in Judy's job description.

Judy was very concerned about the children whom she fed. She got to know a number of them as she helped serve the food in the cafeteria line. She was friendly and encouraged them all "to eat their veggies". She got to know the children with particular health problems and was very conscious of their diets, and made sure that they were helped with any alterations in the menu that they might need. She watched when the children returned their trays and paid attention to what foods they seemed to like, and what was often discarded. She encouraged them to eat better and they all seemed to respect and like her.

Japanese language is very hard to learn for the English speaking population as these languages are so very different from each other. Judy had been taking classes in English for many years. Her classes were the adult education classes offered for free at the high school in the evenings. Judy continued to take English classes over the years as she wanted to improve her reading and writing skills in our language. She would bring short lists of word she did not know (ones she had come across in her reading) to school most every morning. I always stopped in to see her before school started, and she would ask me the meanings of these words. As I had been interested in helping with this, she invited me to come to her adult education class, and perhaps volunteer as a helper. This was a very interesting experience. The ESL (English as a second language) teacher was brilliantly organized. She presented current events at the beginning of the class. She had the students discuss what was in the news. Then she had an instructional session where she taught them about apartment leases, legal situations, special holidays, etc. In her next period of time she had the students read aloud in small groups. In the final part of her lesson they were to asked to do a written assignment. She had three of us who were volunteers. She had the group divided into fourths. She and the three of us sat in smaller groups and helped oversee the reading and help students with their writing. I did not work with Judy's group as the smaller groups were divided by primary languages. I learned a lot from the ESL teacher and enjoyed the international flavor of the class.

Judy joined with some of her friends from Japan to develop a group that would study Japanese dancing. When they became more professional they presented programs of dance and other information from their culture at the local citizens center. Judy helped all of her friends in the group with the sewing and importing of costumes. The performances were well attended and beautifully performed. Judy is now retired. She is still working with her Japanese women's group and still performs. I am still a Christmas card friend to Judy and we have occasional phone conversations.

Chapter Eleven

POST-MORTEM

(Webster's 2nd meaning, "after the event")

After the event of my retirement, which I was unhappy to have, I began working once a week in the same school as a volunteer. The last few years of my teaching I had been working with the "Gifted and Talented Program". The school counselor and I were having a weekly sessions with the students so identified. Part of the regulations of the program was that they were to receive some psychological support once weekly to help them in adjusting to their "gifted and talented" identity. We had instructional sessions that focused on self esteem and personal development. When the counselor moved, I continued working with the students. I had them doing creative writing skills, and deductive reasoning worksheets (as a game), along with some counseling. I felt that my working with the higher achieving students along with the special education students would help the special education students with their self esteem. They would not just be associated with me as a teacher of the handicapped, but also a teacher working at the other end of the spectrum. It did seem to help.

The last two years before I left teaching I had fourth and fifth grade accelerated students groups, and we did creative writing after school. I talked with the principal and we continued the creative writing program for the "Gifted and Talented" students. I went to school one day a week in the morning and saw each grade level group for forty-five minutes each. We focused on the different genres of literature, and twice a year the groups entered a national poetry contest. I have had most all of them get accepted for publishing during the time they spent in my writing program. Over the last few years the population of our school has gradually changed. We have a lot of bi-lingual students and they are not very proficient in language skills for English. I have continued to send their poetry to the contests and they continue to win placement in the anthologies. The difference now is that they are now not identified as "Gifted and Talented". Last year only two of my nineteen students were identified members of that program. I then worked with the more proficient writers, and sometime a student or two that seemed to have a propensity for written expression. A few of the children that came to me for special classes in creative writing also had learning difficulties. Several had dyslexia, several had Aspergers syndrome, and two were moderately autistic.

Currently the school is "unsatisfactory" in its overall evaluation. The principal is on notice to improve and she does not want any students to be removed from class for special groups. They are all to remain "in class" for any additional instruction. I had made arrangements to teach a small group in the back of a regular classroom, but the teacher involved has been relieved of her regular teaching assignment and is now tutoring failing students (*in* their own classrooms with the teacher present) I am at present not able to volunteer there—unless we develop an after school program.

My Volunteer Kids

These were students assigned to my program because of their acknowledged ability in writing or creative expression.

Rubie

A charming and lovely fifth grade girl, named Rubie, graced my program just last year. She was so appreciative that when her teacher let Rubie's group know that I did the work with them without pay, Rubie wrote me a long note of thanks. She also wrote me a number of special poems just about me. I had Rubie the year before when she was in fourth grade. At that time she was making bead necklaces and bracelets as a hobby. She made one of each for me. I kept them in my briefcase so that I would not forget to wear them on Wednesdays when I went to school. Her fourth grade teacher loved her as did all of the teachers who worked with Rubie. She was also the darling of her creative writing group. She had a singular way of making everyone else seem special. This was very helpful to her because of the event that happened last year.

Rubie was absent one week. I was not concerned as it was winter and often different children were out with colds or the flu. I asked about her and her classmates only said that she had been absent for a while, several days in fact. The next Wednesday Rubie returned. She was quieter than usual during the instruction and then, during the writing time, she came over and said quietly, "Dr. Lancer, do you know why I was absent?" I responded that I did not and asked if she had been ill. Her answer was, "No, my sister was murdered". She told me the story and when the students were dismissed, she stayed and talked more about it. Two of her closer friends stayed with her for the conversation. They put their arms around Rubie, very protectively and interspersed supportive comments as we all talked. I told Rubie how very sorry I was and gave her a big hug. Her friends escorted her out of the room as they were almost late for lunch. They left with each girl having her arm around Rubie from either side. The school office staff knew of the event and all were very sorry for Rubie, as she was a favorite throughout the school. Her classroom teacher had gone to Rubie's home, taken a gift for Rubie, and talked with her mother. I was late in finding out about her sister's death and so missed any funeral or visit to the home. I brought a stuffed toy to school for Rubie and wrote a special poem for her. She was extremely appreciative of all the love and concern shown to her from the kids and the adults at her school.

Rubie had had a poem published the year before, and for the spring contest she wrote a poem about her sister. It was selected for publication and I have (with Rubie's permission) included it at the end of this book. The horrific story of her sister death is as follows;

Her older sister (who was in her twenties) had been married to a young man who went astray of the law. I was told about his misdeeds but do not remember the specifics. I think there was theft and drugs involved. The young man fathered two children with his wife, Mary. There was a boy five and a girl four. While he was incarcerated, Mary developed a relationship with another young man. I don't know if she were divorced and then got remarried: Rubie was vague about the legal relationships. Mary had twins with the second partner. Rubie and her mother often babysat with Mary's four children. Rubie especially loved the babies. She and her sister were very close. They often went shopping together and Mary was often at Rubie's home, usually with all four kids.

The first husband was released from prison. Mary was not home on the day that he came to visit the older children that were his. The other man was there and very distressed about someone in his place. Soon after, when Mary was home alone, the children away at a sitter's, the new "husband" came home and confronted Mary. He was apparently enraged with jealousy. Rubie said that her mother told her Mary was drowned. But, she said, "I heard them talking and Mary was also beaten and strangled". The young man had then killed himself.

Rubie said her mother was tending to all four children until after the funeral and until legal situations could be resolved. The father, who had the older children, wanted to gain custody of his kids. It was given to him. The grandparents of the twins (who were only a little more than a year old) told Rubie's mom that they wanted the babies to be where they were most comfortable. They were still grieving over their son and did not see any way to take the custody of the babies. Rubie's mom still has them and she has had to give up her job in order to care for them. I assume that there is some social security funds to help with their support. It is not yet determined if the grandmother will stay home to raise them, or return to work and hire a sitter to care for them.

When I last spoke with Rubie's fifth grade teacher she told me that Rubie was doing very well. She had started middle school. She seemed to be adjusting well, and had returned to her old school to receive a rather high award for math proficiency. She had been given the award in a ceremony for the total school. Her teacher remarked that she did extremely well with her personal tragedy, to then be able to excel in her academics. I am expecting to visit Rubie soon to give her the book of poetry with her poem about her sister.

I Have All Four

One of my most interesting students was a rather large somewhat heavy young man. He had short blonde hair, a perfectly featured face, and a rather distant look in his eye. I was never quite sure when Skyler was looking at me. He did not connect with the students sitting around him at our large conference table where we had our writing class. There were nine students, and when I had finished the introduction, presented the lesson, and started the writing time, all would quietly work on their own. That is, except for Skyler. Early in the fall the writing was about poetry. I gave lessons about form, rhyming, topics, etc., and then read a few poems to the group. The class was then given time to create a poem of their own, using the elements and skills we were studying. Skyler was very insecure about putting anything on paper. He would write a short phrase and then want to read it to me for my approval. He would say "Is this Okay?" and then without hesitating, begin to read. When he was seated at the other end of the conference table, it was very distracting for all the others as they were trying to form ideas of their own. I asked Skyler to sit next to me so that we could consult—quietly. I pointed out that the others were trying to concentrate and needed quiet. He and I needed to talk very softly. I also told the class—as they began complaining—that this was the way that Skyler needed to work. He had to hear his words out loud before he could continue with his writing. They were accepting of Skyler for many of his different behaviors.

Skyler was in a special program for help with his academics, and he was diagnosed as autistic. He had excellent reasoning skills and understood about others' ideas and motivations, when they were explained to him. He did not connect well socially with the other students and did not seem too interested in understanding much about them, only as related to how they responded to him. There was a bully in his regular classroom that housed about four of the members of this writing class. We had discussions on how to handle this bully's aggressive behavior. Skyler could come up with great ideas for responses to the bully's derogatory comments. I am not sure that he used this when he was actually involved in discourse with the bully. The students all were supportive of comments that Skyler made. He did say he was not intimidated by this boy as he, Skyler, was larger and stronger. I made suggestions for the group in handling the bullying and sticking up for each other. From reports that I got, the boys did support each other, except for Skyler. He was always a loner.

Skyler lived with his father. His parents were divorced, but they lived in the same neighborhood. Skyler talked much about his father. I had not seen his dad but the teachers told me he was a rather unusual man. He was very supportive of Skyler and they did not know what kind of work he did. One of them thought that he was an auto mechanic. He was rather hippie-like in his appearance. He had a full beard and quite long hair. Skyler went through a stage of talking a lot about his dad. He was concerned because his step-mom was going to have a baby. He said she was not really his stepmother, as she and his dad were not married. He was concerned because his father had had two other women that lived with him before. The last one had taken things that belonged to Skyler's dad. Skyler said, "She robbed us. I hope this one isn't like her". He seemed quite adult in his observation that his dad had not been making great choices in his partners. He could not remember why the first two left. He was concerned that this union would also not be permanent.

Skyler told me when the baby came and actually shared this news with his class. This is the first time that I saw Skyler trying to be a part of the group. We were all happy for him. We all asked about the baby from time to time and Skyler seemed to like having a little sister. He talked about her often. This was really good progress in his socialization. But then one day he came in quite distraught. His dad and stepmother had had a big "fight" and she moved out—with the baby! Skyler was concerned again about whether or not she would "rob" them. He said he missed the baby. He talked about the baby from time to time, and let us all know when he had a visit from the baby and his step-mother. Skyler had seldom mentioned his real mother even though he went to stay with her often. He seemed more attached to his dad.

It was difficult to pull poetry from Skyler. He had to have approval for each section that he wrote and would often say, "I don't know what should come next". I would reread the start to him and say, "What do you *feel* should come next?" His poems were often quite repetitive and although we were using repetition for effect in poetry, Skyler's repetition was often related to his autism. I often needed to help him interrupt his rhythm and proceed with his thoughts. He did manage to get several acceptable poems completed that could be submitted to the poetry contest that the group all entered.

When the results of the entries were received, there was Skyler's name with those accepted for publication. I think that I was as pleased as Skyler! This was great for him, a real first in his school career. The students needed to have parental permission returned to the publisher and Skyler was a difficult person from whom to get a follow up. I had to go to his home as the deadline for returning signatures was upon us. Skyler's father came to the door. He was very pleased and proud of Skyler, and he was more than happy to sign a permission for publication. He ordered one of the anthologies from the publisher, so that Skyler could have his "published" poem in his own book. I had Skyler in class again the next year and he had another poem accepted. He was seeming more confident and was interacting a little more with his classmates.

Our writing groups were usually forty-five minutes to an hour long. After instruction, and writing time, I would collect the students work and dismiss them with a small piece of hard candy, a Jolly Rancher. One day during the second year of Skyler's being in my group, he asked how many grams of sugar were in the candy. I said, "I don't know. Let's look". I took out the package to read on the label. I told him how many grams were in eight pieces and asked him to do the math. He did and said, "I don't think that is too many". Of course I asked him about his concern, and if he were diabetic. He said he was. Then he said. "I think I got it from my dad. I got my autism and bi-polar from my mom, and I think I got diabetes and ADD from my dad." I repeated the afflictions and asked if he had all of these for sure. "Oh, yes," he responded almost with pride, "I have all four". I was surprised that his parents had burdened him with such information. Maybe it was done in an angry conversation of accusations. I did not know. I do think that he needed to be aware of a blood sugar problem, and knowledge about autism could be helpful if handled correctly. The other ailments did not seem so necessary to have been addressed.

I'm Good At This

One of my fifth grade girls was quite large for her age. She was slightly overweight but mostly she just had large bones. She and two of the other fifth grade girls talked to each other rather roughly, and reported to me that they were good "fighters". They had not had any fights at school and I assumed that it was all just tough talk. Certainly the three of them had some anger issues, more than just what comes from starting to become a teenager. Larissa was from a mixed racial marriage. Her father was black and her mother was Hispanic. Larissa had the tight curly hair from her father and a beautiful evenly colored brown skin from her mother. She had very large dark eyes with long lashes. She was concerned about her appearance and wore very fashionable clothes.

Larissa had a lot of defiance and could take offense when none was intended. A number of times she had lashed out at her classmates when she felt they were disdainful of her. The second time we met she brought a poetry book with some of her work in it. Since she showed it to me at the end of class I asked if I could keep it till the next week to really look at it. She seemed pleased that I was interested. When I returned it, I complimented her on her drawings and mentioned several of the poems. It was not exceptional work, but she was proud. There were two poems that were near her grade level in ability. She was so very proud she said, "I am good at this". She said she was glad that she could be in my special class so she could write some more poetry. She remained rather defiant with her classmates while she was in my program, and there were times when she needed to have situations redefined for her, so she could understand that not every comment was directed to offend her. I would hear reports that she had ended up in the office for confrontations with teachers or other students.

Larissa worked hard in the writing class. She wrote many poems and often would turn in extra work. She really loved writing. The first semester she entered a poem that she had written about being herself. It was well done and got accepted for publishing. The second semester her poem for entry was about being in an apartment with no landscaping. I did help her by suggesting that she let the reader know at the beginning of the poem, why she needed a "secret garden". She put some additional lines on it for her submission. This was great progress for Larissa, as she did not want anyone suggesting to her how something should be done. She was very receptive and very happy when her poem was accepted for publishing a second time. She has gone on to middle school but did stop by and see her old fifth grade teacher twice so far this fall. I do believe that she is beginning to react less angrily.

Chapter Twelve

SUMMARY

(Cross-eyed Bears)

I know that "cross-eyed "is not politically correct these days. But for this story I cannot use "visually impaired", "eye-focus challenged", or some other alternative. In my day people were cross-eyed. I love this little kid story:

A young lad, who had parents who had never taken him to church, was visiting his very conservative grandmother. His grandmother took him to Sunday School for his very first visit. She was anxious about his response and how it had affected him. She asked, "Did you like Sunday School?" "Oh, yes!" he replied happily, "It was fun." "Did you learn anything?" prodded the grandmother. "Yeah," he smiled, "And we sang songs". "What did you sing?" persisted grandma. "A song about a bear". "A bear?" she questioned. "Yeah, a bear, his name was Gladly". "Oh?" grandma was surprised. "Yes, and he was cross-eyed". Grandma was confused. "You sang a song about the bear?" "Yeah, it was cool. We sang 'Gladly, the cross-eyed bear'."

This story is amusing to my family and we often speak of our hindrances, trials, and such as cross-eyed bears. In looking over all my stories of all my students with various impairments, emotional problems, tragic situations, and such, I was impressed to feel that we all have cross-eyed bears. Some are huge like grizzlies, some are more mild like Teddy bears, but all in some way were barriers to our achievements and developments. My kids had physical bears, perceptual bears, emotional bears, and environmental bears. The severity of their obstacles (bears) or the type of obstacles were often the determinate of the child's success.

Allison, with great physical impairment, remained positive, focused, and persevered. Her achievement in learning just one word to employ a two-way communication was a great joy. Melissa with her tragic environmental obstacles, kept trying. And she is still trying to overcome her sad situation. Rene, with the most severe perceptual impairments that I have encountered, worked hard, learned in spite of them, and fulfilled his desire to become an artist. My observations and thoughts about these many obstacles lead me to the conclusion that physical, perceptual, and mental obstacles are more easily dealt with than the emotionally charged obstacles that taint the reason of those affected. I think of poor Phillip who seemingly had no chance. Also, Lisa, who truly wanted to be good enough for "God to choose her" and still made wrong choices. And, I am sure we all consider our own cross-eyed bears, and are grateful when we can overcome the effects of them and sometimes the hindrance itself. I would suppose that most people have some bears that stay with them for their lifetimes, and they continue on doing their very best. I have great hindrances that I try to put aside, and I hope I did my very best with these lovely children about whom I have written.

Chapter Thirteen

HEART

This section of my book is truly the "appendix". I had trouble naming the content of this section of my book after that rather disgusting part of our bodies. These inclosures should surely be entitled the "Heart".

Roseann

I did not write about Roseann. She lost her mother through cancer just a few months before she came to my program. Her following poem was accepted for publishing in a children's poetry anthology. some thirty years ago.

I Miss My Mom

Sometimes I feel alone
When my head hurts,
And I have the fllu,
On a beautiful day,
And a trip to the zoo,
When I get something in my eye,
When there's a rainbow in the sky,

I wish I had my mom
To share
With me.

Where people go
Is where others go,
And everyone goes,
And my mother went there,

Up in the beautiful sky.
I wish she was here
To care
About me.
(Roseann)

Shannon

This first poem by Shannon was published in a poetry anthology for children nearly twenty years ago. I wrote that in high school she received recognition for her poetry reading in a regional contest, and she "lettered" in forensics in high school. She had audio tapes for her reading throughout high school.

Rodeo

Six o'clock, Saturday morning
The snow is falling.
The leaves are crunching.
The breakfast is burned.
The radio is deafening.
The baby is crying.

A redhead comes home
When she should have been home

Hours ago!
Bull-riding blood in her hair,
Calf-hay stuck on her boots,
Mom sends the Rodeo Queen
To her room.
No more Rodeo Queen,
Just a regular redhead
That goes to work
With the tacos
And comes home
And
Goes to bed.
(Shannon)

Buffalo

I run with the Buffalo
Wild and free
With only the wind
Touching me
The heaven above here
The thunder below
Of the great herds of the Buffalo
Soon it will be silent
And the spirits will moan
For there will be
No more Buffalo
The plains will be empty
Where the great beast once stood
Only the bones as a marker to tell
(Shannon)

The Storm

The fall of the rain,
The whisper of the wind,
The fall of the leaves,
Tells me that it's here again.
The grief!
The joy is gone.

It rains harder.
The babies are crying.
Everyone is scared.
The storm gets harder and harder.
The night is filled with sound.

The rain slows down.
The whispers of the wind
Put the babies to sleep.
The ghosts still walk,
But are more silent tonight

Everyone remembers the storm.
In the morning everyone is happy again,
But nobody forgot the storm.
(Shannon)

Jacob

Jacob's intelligence was so incredible that it was almost frightening to read some of his thoughts, knowing they came from such a young child. I had my "learning disability" classes work on their assigned spelling lists. They could then get one hundred percent on their test by the end of the week, and so they could all have some academic excellence. On Mondays after introduction of words from their lists, I had them practice writing skills by making a sentence for the spelling words. I have included some of Jacobs "spelling sentences". Probably, the spelling word in each sentence is one of the more common words!

It is the seventh extruded clown sitting on the buffalo carcass.
September brings wack-o-path flags hanging in Jesse's nose.
Spring makes me say $^&*@ into the megaphone.
It was hard to breathe because the powdered clowns were contaminating the air.
Please close your pajamas.
The red polka-dotted salamander thong is yours.
It costs eight sea shells and a butterfly wing.
He is known for his grimy finger nails and his explosive rubber ducky.
He was crying because the chipmunk ate his brother Timothy.
He eats his pencils and regurgitates them on the floor.
It is coming—it is bad—It is February.
You haven't fed the bologna.
Do not spend more than eight beaver chips at the cloud castle.
The Mona Lisa probably thinks its not always easy to hold that smile.
He drove around the wet slimy pond two times.
The emperor of Kadoodoo sat in a decorative golden carriage by the shore.
The Miller's pet morops growled at the waxing moon.
The caravan of camels stops as the shooting star streaks across the northern sky.
She unfolded the laser lemon envelope brought here by the sugar swan.
The twisted adventure of life is sparking an idea with every random turn.
The strongest of the ants lives in a Pepsi can in Sheboygan.
They served seven courses at the bull frogs' feast.
On another planet a million urns sang for practice.
One pleasureful fairy equals five people.
She was the fifteenth gnome with a beard.
The forty purple slippers lined the mushroom house.
Only orange makes us be ourselves.
He lived on the eastern side of my thumbnail.
The frog's kitchen was filled with elaborate paintings of angels in flight.
The blue kites jumped on Shaleen like a trampoline.
The pages of the book grew human arms.

Dawn

The light
Streams across the night sky
Illuminating the cold black heavens
Turning the mountains pink,
Bringing life to the world
And beaming warmth
To each and every person,
Starting the day
In a beautiful show
Of light and color.
(Jacob)

The Beach

A sparkling wave crashes down
Singing a song
As the crystal sea dances to its tune.

The song that holds seagulls up
And makes the sand sparkle.

The song that nature
Has had a million years to perfect.

The song of the beach.
(Jacob)

Dream Maze

In the dream maze
I will venture in the places where no one goes.
Beyond the night-mares,
I will journey to the castle that lies within,
Through the poison flower gardens,
Across the jungle-gym in the sky,
Through the steaming acid river.

And I will defeat the dark dragon,
For I am Truth.
And I will at last
Enter the castle of the heart.
(Jacob)

Final Say

I must make, at the last, a final attack toward what is happening in our education system. We teachers are given numerous and ponderous "inservices" to teach us how we should be teaching. These are usually by some self-appointed expert who is being endorsed by an even less expert principal or administrative guru. A (not brief enough) sojourn of these intellectuals (?) for several years produced an non-clever way to teach kids how to do a paragraph. The recipe was:

A statement (naming the topic)

First (a complete sentence—or more defining of—or description of the topic)

Secondly (another sentence to further describe the topic)

Thirdly (IF you can get another aspect of their thoughts)

All in All (a statement summarizing the ideas) or use, In Summary, or Finally

I recently learned that this same "recipe" is also used in China, and other countries to unify the process and further define a "paragraph". I was annoyed at first, and then horrified to see a Mothers Day card done by a fourth grader that read:

"Dear Mom, I love you.
First, you buy me clothes.
Secondly, you fix my meals.
Thirdly, you clean the house.
All in All, I love you,
Happy Mothers Day."

Please note what this instruction did to the above genius Jacob (certainly described by his own writing with his amazing creativity). I hope no more experts have helped Jacob to write! This was a certain method to stifle any creativity. Here is what he produced in his regular classroom after a class field trip to a concert, and an assignment (in *his* classroom) to tell about the experience. (in the way the teacher tells the class to make a paragraph).

"Today we went to the symphony concert. I believed this was an enjoyed experience for many reasons.

First, I enjoy classical music. I found the concert relaxing.

Second, I enjoyed other students attending the concert. There were some very interesting children there.

Third I enjoyed watching the musicians. I believe the musicians are interesting to watch.

In conclusion, I enjoyed the symphony." (Jacob)

Jacob wrote numerous stories, every bit as interesting as his very imaginative spelling sentences and creative poetry. What a poor example he gives with unneeded *super* instruction!

Students In My Volunteer Classes

These are recent poems from my volunteer teaching time. These have all been accepted for publication and printed in a poetry anthology called "A Celebration of Poets" by Creative Communications, a publishing company out of Utah. They print school children's poetry from around the country. These are all by children about whom I have written. They are not learning disabled, but several of them have other problems interfering with their progress.

My Sister's Picture

My sister's picture reminds me of her.
I don't get to see her anymore
Because she died on January 15, 2011.
But her picture reminds me of her smile.
How I remember seeing her with a great smile.
Every time I saw her she would smile all the while.
Her picture reminds me of the great times we had.
It reminds me of what she always wore.
It reminds me of when we used to go to the mall.
It reminds me when we used to laugh.
(Rubie)

Snowflakes

I looked from the window to the outside
I saw big bright snowflakes glide.
I zipped my cozy, warm fuzzy coat
And wrapped a scarf at my throat.
I went outside to play
With the fresh wet snow.
Flakes landed on my frizzy hair.
And had a sparkly glow.

I saw the ground getting a blanket of white.
Then on my trampoline, I played till night.
All the cold freezing snow on my shoes,
Covering my feet, I'm glad they were not bare!
My feet might get cold, but I'm not going to freeze
While no one is there.
"Now what am I going to do with a cold?'
I guess I will have the chills
(So I've been told.)
And stay in the bed
The whole snowflake day.
(Rubie)

Halloween

Black, spooky, scary cats creeping without a sound,
Witches, goblins, and skeletons laughing on the ground,
Witches, warlocks, sorcerers casting spells
Up and down and all around,
Bloody scary zombies running up and down,
Gargoyles, bats, and ghosts flying and screaming
In the sky, can be found.
Spooky, scary screams coming from the ground,
Boy, oh boy, what a spooky sound!
Mummies, vampires and werewolves rising from the ground,
Howling, screaming and running all the way through town,
Pumpkins smiling without a frown.
Halloween, Halloween—it is going to be fun!
Darn it, Darn, it is almost done.
(Skyler)

Me

Me,
Me, only me,
No one can take my place.
The things I love
Mythology, reading, my special space.
Back away!
Here I come with my stuffed bear.
I know that I look tough
But I'm just an ordinary girl
With feelings (more than enough).

They say, "Here she comes
With her stuffed teddy bear.
But while she's a giant, so tall,
Hovering over us all,
We should not care.
But how come she has
A stuffed teddy bear?
(Larissa)

The Secret Garden

Cramped up in an apartment so small
With no trees, no flowers,
But a little key can change that all.
There—the tiny door—full of flowers
Shall be a secret garden,
Full of bunnies, deer and such,
Full of bushes and pines.
Oh wonder!—a magic!
All you have to do is imagine.
(Larissa)

www.ingramcontent.com/pod-product-compliance
Lightning Source LLC
LaVergne TN
LVHW041807060526
838201LV00046B/1160